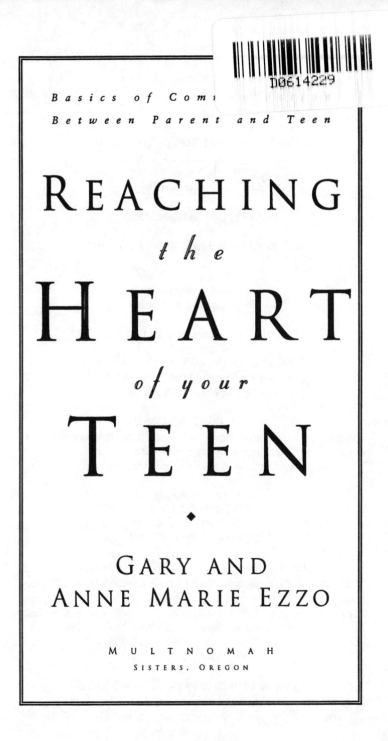

Basics of Com...
Between Parent and Teen

REACHING
the
HEART
of your
TEEN

◆

GARY AND
ANNE MARIE EZZO

MULTNOMAH
SISTERS, OREGON

REACHING THE HEART OF YOUR TEEN

published by Multnomah Books
a part of the Questar publishing family

© 1997 by Gary and Anne Marie Ezzo

International Standard Book Number: 1-57673-022-0

Editor: Shari MacDonald
Copyeditor: Candace McMahan
Cover Design: David Carlson

Printed in the United States of America

Unless otherwise indicated, all Bible quotations are
from the *New King James Version* (NKJV)
© 1984 by Thomas Nelson, Inc.

For information:
QUESTAR PUBLISHERS, INC.
POST OFFICE BOX 1720
SISTERS, OREGON 97759

Library of Congress Cataloging-in-Publication Data:
Gary Ezzo. Reaching the heart of your teen/by Gary and Anne Marie Ezzo.
p.cm. Includes bibliographical references. ISBN 1-57673-022-0 (alk. paper)
1. Parent and teenager. 2. Parent and teenager--Religious aspects--Christianity.
3. Parenting 4. Adolescence. I. Ezzo, Anne Marie. II. Title.
HO799.15.E95   1997   96-46703
649'.125--dc21   CIP

97 98 99 00 01 02 03 04 —10 9 8 7 6 5 4 3 2 1

Dedicated to

Harold and Evelyn Duff.

One weekend so many years ago.

ACKNOWLEDGMENTS

We are indebted to a number of friends, colleagues, seminary professors, and students who, through encouragement and critical review of each chapter, have added clarification and insight. And to every one of our fellow Growing Families International leaders, we offer a special thanks for their faithfulness and sense of urgency.

We also owe a special debt of gratitude to a host of families who prayed us through the completion of this text. We want to especially thank Jeff and Sharon Secor for their ministry commitment to struggling teens and single parents and for their ongoing encouragement to finish this project. Also, we wish to acknowledge Gary and Laurie Price, John and Holly Angle, Nick and Sharon Carter, Greg and Diane Roehr, Tim and Susan Howard, all who offer hope to many families because of the wonderful testimony of their own teenagers. We wish to thank Scott Shald for granting us permission to use the "Cat Street" story in our first chapter. A special thanks to Pastors Robert Boerman and Dave Maddox for their theological suggestions and contributions.

TABLE OF CONTENTS

INTRODUCTION

When writing to express an idea, an author looks for words that
will tie his thoughts together in a concise, coherent bundle. He
does his best to use terms that will make his plea or point understood. But like life itself, which confounds our desire for fairy tale
endings, so do books about family renewal defy the use of simple
categories. It will always be much easier to talk about healthy families and blissful parent-teen relationships than to achieve them.
But please hear and believe this: Many healthy families exist. And
within these pages, we will share with you the guiding principles
that helped countless numbers of families *achieve this status.*

We are challenged by the variety of circumstances faced by
moms and dads who will pick up this book. Some parents are
deeply troubled—troubled to the point of despair. Many are
overwhelmed by the feeling that something has gone dreadfully
wrong. Others are berated by an inner voice that relentlessly
chants, "You are a failure." Pain is ever with these parents, and
the prospect of family renewal and friendship with an unman-
ageable teen seems nothing more than an impossible dream.
They are not alone in their discouragement.

As young parents, we heard how awful the teen years would
be—a full-time headache marked by impossible communication, peer-dependent children, rebellious behavior, and the end
of domestic peace. The warnings were endless: "If you're too
strict, your children will rebel." "If you hold them to a standard,
they will reject your values." "If you insist on compliance, you
will only get opposition." "Enjoy your kids when they are young
because it is not going to last!"

Dissatisfied but not surprised by the prevailing non-
Christian view of adolescence, we sought encouragement from
within the Church. If there was any basis of hope, we reasoned,

surely the Christian community would provide it.

Yet we found many "in-church" parents dealing with their own teen problems. We hopefully suggested that maybe we could do something as parents to avoid rebellion, drug use, and experimentation with sex by our teens. The response we received was one of frowns and glares from war-torn souls who would roll their eyes and offer the timeless warning: "Just you wait."

We did wait. What we experienced with our teenage children was just the opposite of what was predicted by these prophets of pessimism. Looking back now, we wouldn't trade those teen years for anything. They were not a disappointment much less a disaster. They were delightful years—not perfect, but delightful nonetheless. We did not experience rebellion, sassy talk, doors slamming in defiance, threats to run away, or experimentation with drugs or sex.

Not only was this period free of such dominant negatives, it produced many positives. We were four individuals growing in our relationships. While accepting each other's human frailties, each one of us moved toward a greater love and loyalty within the special bond we call "family."

This book is not just our story; it is the story of many families who have experienced the joy of friendship with their teens. Although healthy families appear to be a minority within our culture, we believe it is time that our voices be heard as an alternative to the disparaging message of the age. The stereotyping of teenagers as hopelessly stress-ridden, rebellious, anti-parent, and hormone-controlled might reflect more accurately society's ills than its *will*.

At the same time we do not dare boast about our accomplishments. We can give you satisfying food for thought, as well as practical helps for building, maintaining, or even restoring parent-teen relationships. But be assured, no family reaches a healthy condition by its own power. At the core of every healthy parent-teen relationship there is a spiritual dimension that cannot be minimized. We serve a great God who is neither offended by our shortcomings nor weary of our cries for help. He does not grow impatient because we have lost our way; He comes to us in time of need. Yes, if you need to, shout out just as Peter did on the sea, "Lord, save me!" He will come to save your family, to guide and direct you in His way. God is worthy of our hope; He alone brings renewal.

Please note that in the following pages, the word *we* refers to the collective insights of both of us, Gary and Anne Marie. When referring to the experiences of just one partner, we have told the story from a third person perspective in order to avoid confusion about who is referred to by the word *I*.

The following chapters outline what God has taught us, as well as many other families, about reaching the heart of a teen. Be encouraged.

Gary and Anne Marie Ezzo
Los Angeles, California

PART I

WHAT YOU NEED

to know about

TEEN REBELLION

CHAPTER ONE

Caught Between Joy and Pain

Among the Mundugumor people of New Guinea, there is a firm belief that children born with the umbilical cord wrapped around their necks are gifted by nature as artists. In this way, the Mundugumor society has connected two completely unrelated aspects of nature—a condition of birth and an ability to paint intricate designs on pieces of wood and stone. This belief is so woven into the fabric of social thought that people within the tribe who are born with the natural ability to paint, but had normal, uneventful births, seek out any trade but art.

Such social conditioning is not completely unknown in our own society. Like the Mundugumor people, many in our culture automatically connect two unrelated subjects—teenagers and rebellion—then act on the belief that adolescence is a time of inevitable conflict. But is that really the case?

How would you describe the teen years? George Bernard Shaw once said, "Youth is a wonderful thing. What a crime to waste it on children." Mark Twain said that if he could, he would live his life over until he reached the age of fifteen…then he would drown.

A quick survey would most likely find parents using terms such as "difficult," "very stressful," and "tumultuous" to describe the experience of parenting teens. The American society believes that parents and their teenagers will do battle. Pain, misery, and sorrow are accepted as a normal expression of family life in post-modern America. As we close out this century, teenage rebellion is widely seen as a normal—even healthy—aspect of family life. In fact, according to some psychologists, a lack of teenage rebellion is a signal that something is terribly wrong with a child.

We are well aware that most contemporary schools of parenting believe in the inevitability of the "storm and stress" years. Let us say at the very start, however, that we do not. Our message is very positive, upbeat, and exciting and comes with plenty of encouragement. We want parents to look forward to the fun-filled years of adolescence. Parents today have every reason to hope for and experience strong, positive, healthy, and lasting relationships with their teens.

The fundamental problem with most descriptions of the parent-teen experience is just that—they are simply *descriptions*. Statistics, surveys, and other clinical studies assume the validity of the power of observation. The process works this way: Statistics tell us what is common; what is common then becomes what is normal; normal is deemed inevitable; and finally, what is seen as inevitable is labeled healthy. Yet such logic is horribly flawed. "Common" and "normal" are not interchangeable *concepts* as possibly *realities*. It is not our intention in this book to tell you what merely occurs in many homes, but to offer you hope of what can be. Yes, hope.

HIDDEN TREASURES TODAY

Back in the early '70s, missionary friends living in Hong Kong often spent Sunday afternoons visiting a place locals called "Cat Street." It was at this Chinese flea market that visitors could rummage through the discards of nearby residents, in search of unknown treasures.

One day they came upon a room-divider screen with several panels which folded accordion-style. The center panels contained a mural depicting a scenic view of the Great Wall of China, while the outer panels contained Chinese characters. It was obvious that the screen had been poorly cared for. It might have been pretty at one time, but the years of grime and smoke had taken their toll. The glass within the mural's frames was clouded. The fabric looked stained and rotted. Still, the family took a fancy to the discarded piece and decided to clean it up.

At home they wiped off the grime. To their surprise, they found that the mural beneath the glass was actually a fine piece of embroidery created by a skilled craftsman! With great excitement, they worked to remove the embroidered panels from their frames. The father cautiously removed the wooden back of the first panel. The family was struck with amazement at what was revealed: The color of the embroidery threads exploded with brilliance, showing the richness of the original tapestry. Where it was protected and sheltered within the framework, the magnificence of the original work had not deteriorated.

Frame by frame the family cleaned the screen. Each panel revealed the same quality of artwork, and collectively they formed a majestic scene of the Great Wall of China. Next came the panels of Chinese characters. The father asked the Chinese housekeeper to interpret their meaning. She responded by giving them the following translation:

> It takes strong marriages to build strong families.
> It takes strong families to build strong people.
> It takes strong people to build a strong nation.

Like our friends with their grime-covered screen, many parents with teenage children feel their family is tainted by the world and dulled by time. For some, the original sketch of a beautiful family is so faded that it cannot even be imagined. Maybe your family looks like the outside of the mural in this story. But in this book, we would like to unveil what lies beneath the stains and grime. Just beneath the surface lies a beautiful piece of God's handiwork that waits to be discovered by your loving eyes and caring hands. With God's help, faith and a little work, you will be able to discover its secrets.

FAITH, NOT FEAR

Parents today have little reason to believe a beautiful relationship lies waiting to be discovered during their children's teen years. Journalists and school counselors quote statistics about drug use, sexual activity, abortions, and violence that can leave us gasping, "Is it really that bad?" As if to confirm our worst fears, hardly a day passes without our local newspaper covering at least one story about a gang-related incident, the arrest of a teen for a violent crime, or the decline of SAT scores.

Some of us respond with hope-filled bravado or condemnation. "That won't ever happen in our family." "The problem is, parents just don't love their kids or take care of them." "If any of my kids ever did that, I'd put an end to it real quick." But somewhere deep inside, the fear that it could happen to us whispers, "You're not a perfect parent. What makes you think your kids will be different?"

As parents, we felt a similar fear twenty years ago. But as we experienced our children's teen years, and as we worked with the thousands of parents who attend our seminars, God showed us that parenting takes faith, not fear—faith to live before our children what we believe, faith to trust and act upon the principles He has outlined in His Word, faith to believe God honors rightness and loves our children more than we ever could.

We'll tell you up front: Reaching the heart of your teen will take work, diligence, and patience. Most important, it will require taking a new and honest look at yourself. The cycle of change begins with parents—with their hearts and minds. Yet the rewards are far-reaching. Our desire for this book is not to make you a better parent or your teen a better son or daughter, but to help all of you become better people—people who know Christ, people who understand His mind, purpose, and plan for enduring relationships. These are the threads from which God weaves strong families.

TWO REALMS

Clay and Beth's two sons and two daughters experienced their share of adolescent ups and downs. Though their youngest, Holly, struggled with accepting her looks, she did not turn to girl-hunting guys. Though Rob, their oldest, dealt with pride when he became captain of the basketball team, he did not turn to the alcohol commonly used by the "jock" set.

Each of their children had to confront issues during adolescence. In each struggle, they did not turn from their parents and their values but instead turned to them. They made choices that brought lifelong joy to Clay and Beth.

Bob and Meg raised three boys while pastoring a small country church. During adolescence, their sons also faced difficulties. Jason's academic problems frequently put him in classes with undisciplined kids. By ninth grade, he'd taken on their belligerent attitude. Their second son, Ryan, started using drugs after years of shyness. When their last son began to experiment with homosexuality, Bob and Meg's sorrow and intense feelings of failure caused them to leave the ministry. The joy and high hopes they had had for each of their sons were buried beneath incredible pain.

These two families represent opposite ends on a parent-teen relationship continuum. On one end is a joy-filled, positive relationship. On the other end is a relationship filled with conflict and pain. As parents, we fit somewhere on the continuum with each of our children.

Joy, Rapport +_____ - *Pain, Conflict*

Society would tell us that the negative end of the relationship continuum is normal for adolescence. Contemporary clinicians, who reflect the biases of popular culture, would have us believe that an adolescent storm must inevitably come blowing down on families like a frigid north wind, spreading discord and turmoil in its wake.

Of course, no family is utterly free of conflict. Likewise, even the strongest family experiences discouragement. Sinless perfection awaits us in heaven. But that is the future. The here and now requires us to do battle with contemporary secular wisdom, which gives birth to fatalism, and finally to despair. In Christ, we are no longer a slave to sin (Romans 5:12–19). The believer lives in the realm of the Spirit where there is life, joy, and forgiveness.

Rebellion is an issue that God deals with from the Garden of Eden in Genesis to the final judgment in Revelation. Each time, God exposes rebellious behavior as a heart problem. That is why He says in Proverbs 4:23, "Keep your heart with all diligence, for out of it spring the issues of life." That is why He searches our hearts and speaks of foolishness being bound in them.

After her husband died, Angie was left alone to raise four children, ages eight to twelve. For five years, she experienced the joy of loving relationships with her adolescent sons and daughters. Then her youngest reached thirteen. For the next two years, she faced drugs, promiscuity, running away, a treatment center, counseling, support groups, and even attempted suicide.

The pain of her daughter's rebellion and the consequences she would face far exceeded the grief Angie had felt at her husband's death. She wanted to turn from God, to turn from the unanswered prayers and fasting. But she could not. God was her life. As she crawled into His lap and pounded her fists on His chest and wept uncontrollably on His shoulder, bit by bit God began to expose the failed relationship that lay beneath her daughter's rebellion.

This revelation broke her spirit. It drained every ounce of parenting pride built up with her three other children. It caused her to hear the whisper, "Repent, repent."

Angie says, "God did not let me cross into the never-ending guilt of my daughter's choices, but He did make me deal with my failed responsibilities as her mother."

Though our children are free-standing moral agents and must answer to God for their choices, it is important to note that there is more than a causal relationship between parent and child. The apostle Paul addresses this dynamic when he warns parents not to exasperate their children (Ephesians 6:4). Angie learned that when a child sins, responsibility falls on both child and parent. She also learned about the power of God's grace. At the low point of her relationship with her daughter, Angie turned to God and took responsibility for her actions as a parent. As she did, she learned that with the Christian, there is no final failing. God's children are never beyond a new and fresh start. Our heavenly Father picks us up, brushes us off, and sets us on a new course.

THE TWO-EDGED SWORD

No one who believes in Christian charity wishes to inflict more pain upon those who are grieving over their children's troublesome choices in life. Such compassion leads many of us to speak these words: "It's OK; it is not your fault; you are not to blame." Yet these reassurances are like the blade of a two-edged sword. The sweeping cut that so neatly divides personal responsibility from happenstance, at the same time severs hope from despair. If pure motives without right methods render us blameless for what we do or say, then we have no hope of recovering from destructive patterns of parenting. But this is not the case. We, as parents, must know that our actions do have an impact.

Thus, words intended to extend loving encouragement may offer false comfort. We do no favors for this generation nor for future generations by consoling with words of goodwill while shielding the truth from those we wish to help.

The good news is that parents can and do make a difference because God makes a difference. God can "restore to you the years that the swarming locust has eaten" (Joel 2:25). Angie knows the truth of this. Recently, she returned from a conference. Coming off the plane, she saw her now-married youngest daughter waiting to greet her. After a big hug, Angie asked, "Didn't you have to work the graveyard shift last night?"

"Yes," her daughter answered. "But I set my alarm. I didn't want you to come home to an empty airport."

Though painful, it had been worth letting God expose the failed core of Angie's parenting.

Secular and Christian counselors alike recognize the significant damage done to society and to an individual when personal responsibility is undermined. We live in a day marked by a victimization epidemic. The truth is, in most people-to-people situations, we are at once victim *and* agent.

Angie's daughter was a victim of Angie's poor parental choices. Yet it is equally true that she was an agent of sinful choice as well. A balanced, biblical view would have Angie taking responsibility for her actions as mom before a holy and loving God. It would

also have her daughter doing the same. Somehow, in the conflu-
ence of mother and daughter activity, each will have responsibility
for her own actions, in some ways responsible for the life of the
other, yet each will stand before God unable to shift the blame of
sin to the other.

FACING OUR REALITY

As we confront our hearts, we'll need to look at our ideas about
adolescence, our pasts, our parenting styles, and elements that
improve and maintain relationships. But first, we must take an
honest look at our current relationships.

In order to help you, we've put together forty questions that
are designed to assess your parent-teen relationships. Providing
honest answers to these questions won't be easy. From hundreds
of questionnaires completed by parents across the country, we've
discovered that the families with a "healthy" public reputation
tended to be harder on themselves, earning scores that did not
reflect their real situations. Conversely, struggling families tended
either to underrate the seriousness of their problems or to con-
tradict themselves. Some answered, "Yes, my son is on drugs," but
also answered, "Yes, my son is a strong Christian."

It hurts to give answers that drive home the reality of a poor
or struggling relationship between you and your teen. But there
is also great hope in beginning the process. In order to gain opti-
mum help, please be as honest as you can.

The scores at the conclusion of the test represent actual read-
ings from families who have both a private and public reputation
as being:

1. *Strong families with healthy parent-teen relationships;*
2. *Surviving families who could benefit from improvement and
who may experience significant problems in the future;*

*3. Struggling families whose parent-teen relationships are charac-
terized by serious conflict.*

The test is designed simply to provide you with an objective
point of reference. Your final score will help you evaluate where
you stand. The test is not meant to encourage or discourage you
or other parents (although both may happen), but to provide a
starting point for improvement. Remember, a stronger relationship with your teen lies ahead.

ONE FINAL NOTE OF ENCOURAGEMENT

Before you begin, let us remind you of the remarkable freedom and
hope that comes with honesty. Bible scholars tell us that the term
confession means to "say the same thing as." It is critical for us to
understand that turning from a destructive pattern to a life-giving
pattern of living begins with a bold and thoughtful look at reality.

We want to encourage you not to fear that process. The door
to healing is unlocked by the key marked "honesty." Remember,
just on the other side of that door is a merciful Father. There will
be no better time to begin. So go ahead and commit your heart
to the Lord, take the test once for each teen in your home, and
get ready to begin the process of healing your relationship with
your teen!

FAMILY REALITY TEST

This test is divided into two sections, each with a different rating
scale. Please note the difference when you reach the second section. After completing both sections, add the scores and total the
results as indicated. If for some reason a question does not apply,
make an educated guess. For personal enlightenment, consider
taking the test on behalf of your own parents. How do you think
they would answer these questions about you?

SECTION ONE

Write your responses in the spaces adjacent to each question in this section, basing your answers on the following 1 to 5 scale:

1 = *This represents our teen or our relationship.*
2 = *This usually represents our teen or our relationship.*
3 = *Sometimes this is true of our teen or our relationship, but just as often, it is not.*
4 = *This is not usually true of our teen or our relationship.*
5 = *This rarely, if ever, is true of our teen or our relationship.*

1. ___Our parent-teen communication is characterized by very few limitations. We can talk about anything.
2. ___Our teen looks forward to special family times when it is just us together.
3. ___Our teen's friends consider our family a fun family to be with.
4. ___Our teen considers us to be a good source of counsel.
5. ___Our teen can accept no for an answer without blowing up.
6. ___Peer pressure has less influence on our teen than we do.
7. ___Our teen is interested in what is going on in our lives.
8. ___When our teen comes home late, we know he or she will have a legitimate reason.
9. ___Our teen would be one of the sources of counsel that we would seek in time of crisis.
10. ___When we have a disagreement with our teen, we make up quickly without harboring a grudge.
11. ___Our teen knows that if we wrong him or her in any way, he or she can count on an apology from us.
12. ___If we were running late and left the dinner dishes on the table, our teen would probably clean the table, wash the dishes, and put them away.

13. ___Our teen considers us to be fair and flexible.
14. ___Our teen accepts criticism, evaluates it, and is willing to talk about it.
15. ___Our teen considers us to be part of his or her inner circle of best friends.
16. ___Our teen picks up after himself or herself.
17. ___If our teen had a choice, he or she would choose us to be his or her parents.
18. ___Our friends enjoy our teen.
19. ___Our teen has his or her own quiet time with the Lord. We don't have to prompt him or her.
20. ___Our teen feels appreciated by us.

Now add up all of the numbers you placed in the blanks above, and enter the total score in the blank below.

Section One Score _____

SECTION TWO

Write your responses in the blanks adjacent to each question in this section, basing your answers on the following 5 to 1 scale.

5 = *Always true, or this is very representative of our teen, his or her feelings, our feelings, or our relationship.*

4 = *Often the case, or this is usually representative of our teen, his or her feelings, our feelings, or our relationship.*

3 = *Sometimes this is true, but just as often, it is not.*

2 = *This happens, but not often. Or this is not usually representative of our teen, his or her feelings, our feelings, or our relationship.*

1 = *This is rarely, if ever, true of our teen or our relationship.*

1. ___When we ask our teen to do something, we always seem to end up in a power struggle.

2. ___Our teen prefers spending more time with his or her friends than with our family.

3. ___Our teen will often agree with what we say, but then do what he or she wants.

4. ___Our teen is easily influenced by his or her peers, trendy styles, or behaviors.

5. ___Setting limits on our teen doesn't do any good. He or she ignores them all.

6. ___Our teen cannot wait to grow up and leave our home.

7. ___Our teen is not sought out as a baby sitter.

8. ___We don't feel confident in our teen's ability to make wise, age-appropriate decisions for himself or herself.

9. ___If we get into an argument, our teen may not talk to us for a couple of days.

10. ___If it weren't for sports or the weather, we probably wouldn't have anything to talk about with our teen.

11. ___We're fearful that our teen is experimenting or has experimented with drugs.

12. ___Our teen has little interest in spiritual things.

13. ___Our teen's taste in clothing and hairstyle is the opposite of ours.

14. ___If we were going away for the weekend, I don't think we could trust our teen to stay home alone.

15. ___Our teen puts stress on the whole family.

16. ___We are fearful that if we place too many demands on our teen, he or she will run away.

17. ___Our teen physically threatens us.

18. ___We're fearful that our teen is sexually active or even promiscuous.

19. ___Our teen has the attitude that everyone else can pick up after him or her.

20. ___Our teen thinks we are overly critical of him or her.

Section Two Score_____

Section One Score_____

Grand Total _____

Compare your score to the numbers posted under the Family Profile Summary.

FAMILY PROFILE SUMMARY

40 - 60 Very healthy parent-teen relationship.

61 - 80 Healthy parent-teen relationship with minor problems.

81 -115 OK-to-weak parent-teen relationship. There are some behavioral concerns that if not corrected, can lead to struggles and conflict.

116-140 Weak parent-teen relationship characterized mostly by conflict.

141-170 Barely tolerable parent-teen relationship.

171-190 Parent-teen relationship is nonexistent.

Name of Teen _____

Score _____

Name of Teen _____

Score _____

Name of Teen _____

Score _____

CHAPTER TWO

What Is Rebellion?

Computers are amazing instruments. As we type out these chapters, there is a direct relationship between the buttons our fingers punch and the figures that appear on the screen. Hit another button, AND THE TYPE CHANGES. HIT ANOTHER BUTTON, *and the type changes again.* There is a direct relationship between the buttons we touch and what does or does not appear on the screen.

Some parents view teen rebellion in much the same way: Rebellion just happens. It is inevitable. Parents may not fully understand the cause and effect, but they believe that when certain "buttons" are punched in a child's life—presto, out comes rebellion. It is this perspective that we wish to expose as the worst sort of parenting error.

As the parents of two teenagers and one grade schooler, Bill and Teresa knew what it was like to have some bad days. But when their oldest son started to rebel, they knew they were facing much more than a series of bad days. Something was very wrong.

As the trouble continued, friends who asked, "How are the kids?" triggered a rush of pain. Bill would say nothing, while Teresa told about soccer and school pictures—anything but the

weekly arguments, late-night battles over curfews, and delin-
quent friends. Only a few of Teresa's closest friends heard the real
story. In an effort to help, they said things like "Don't worry. It's
just all the hormone changes taking place within him" or "He's
just trying his independence. It will be OK."

HOW DID WE GET HERE?

Bill and Teresa will never argue the fact that at unprecedented
rates teenagers are rebelling against all authority—most pain-
fully against their parents. Neither will they minimize it by saying it's just disagreement. They know there's a big difference
between the terms *disagreement* and *rebellion*.

Disagreement refers to a difference of opinion. *Rebellion*
denotes acts and attitudes intended to change or overthrow family
government and replace it with self-government—a concept
incompatible with family harmony. To be in a protracted state of
rebellion is to be in a state of war.

Bill and Teresa do have questions, though. Why did their son
rebel in the first place? Was it due to hormones, a desire for independence, or a natural and predictable process of growth? To
what extent did they encourage or discourage the storm and
stress of adolescence? Is rebellion a natural control mechanism of
adolescence?

We can assure Bill and Teresa that rebellion is not just an
unavoidable side effect of adolescence. But if this is the case, then
what *is* rebellion? A careful study of biblical text has led us to this
definition: Rebellion is plainly a heart issue, a tendency and condition of our humanity. Scripture says:

•It is man saying no to God, His ways, and His precepts
(Romans 3:18).

•It is the foolishness that is bound up in the heart of the child
(Proverbs 22:15).

•It is the absence of wisdom ruling the moment (Proverbs 1:7; 26:12).

•It is plainly a condition of our fallen humanity (Psalm 51:5).

In 1904, G. Stanley Hall, a psychologist, theorized a link between adolescent rebellion and the onset of puberty and hormone release. This was a radical suggestion then. Since that time, our society has searched for answers apart from the wisdom of Scripture. This quest has led to the popular belief that teen rebellion is isolated and somehow different from the rebellion of adults or young children. Social scientists have theorized, described, debated, and categorized the problem into four classifications. A brief examination of these theories may shed some light on what you believe to be the cause or causes of your teen's rebellion.

HORMONES

The Trigger Theory

No parents who have watched their son with skinny legs and big feet play basketball or watched their daughter worry about when to start wearing a bra, would deny that biological changes have a great impact upon their children. Supporters of the hormone-induced rebellion theory, however, take this one step further. They suggest that the awkwardness of physical maturity along with hormonal changes substantially increase a teen's tendency to rebel.

As we close this century, an inordinate and unsubstantiated amount of blame continues to be placed on the influence of hormones. But are the defiant acts and rebellious mood swings we witness really set in motion by forces of nature at the onset of puberty?

Actually, hormonal changes in the endocrine system begin in children at about age seven, not at twelve, as is commonly believed. This new growth period marks the end of a hormonal suppression set in place soon after birth and the beginning of many years of glandular arousal. At age seven, the gonadotropin hormone levels begin to rise in both boys and girls. The results are more readily seen in girls.

Have you ever wondered why your nine-year-old daughter can change moods overnight, sometimes becoming emotionally irrational? If she spells a word wrong on her English report, she sobs, "I can't do this!" She becomes more snippy toward her siblings. This behavior is evidence of hormones at work long before the teen years begin.

This mind-set begins with what many affectionately call "the terrible twos." It is assumed that there is a bitterness that comes with being a two-year-old child. The same presupposition is made regarding rebellion and the teen years.

Jim and Lois often excused the rebellious spirit of their teenage daughter with the simple refrain "It's her hormones again." That excuse allowed them to walk away from their responsibility to give their daughter the guidance her rebelliousness was crying out for. Slowly, after working with her and her parents, we began to see her turning back to the sweet spirit she'd exhibited before turning thirteen.

The Body Reality

An excess or gross deficiency of one or more of the hormones produced by the glands of the endocrine system can also affect personality. A hyperthyroid condition, for example, can make a child nervous, excited, jumpy, restless, and overactive. A hypothyroid condition causes children to be lethargic, unresponsive, dissatisfied, even depressed. But these are the exceptions, not the norm. And while such imbalances may explain poor behavior but does not legitimize it.

Hormones may affect personality but not morality. The theoretical link between hormones and changes in teen behavior is measurable, but to link hormone levels and teenage rebellion is successfully unfounded and biblically untenable. Glandular surges do not cause children to lie, steal, cheat, be disrespectful, or wander away from their relationships with their parents. In a nutshell, hormones may affect the human body but not the human heart. They may exacerbate already weak relationships, but they don't create them as suggested by modern theory. At worst, hormones have an indirect effect on relationships.

For example, your fourteen-year-old son starts to pay more attention to his grooming and appearance in public because of his attraction to the opposite sex. Trouble brews when his peers' choices in music and hairstyle conflict with your preferences or when he wants to go out with the gang and you want him to stay home and finish his school project. The battle begins, and back and forth you go. Please note, though, that the problem is rooted in values, not an increase in testosterone.

A fifteen-year-old girl retains fluids during her menses and feels bloated. Becoming dissatisfied with her appearance, she pushes herself into a semi-starvation pattern of eating. Her parents forbid this type of dietary behavior, insisting that she eat balanced meals. Tension builds up, and daily arguments ensue. The daughter declares, "You don't understand! You don't love me!"

In this scenario and hundreds like it, only the names of the participants change. Again, please note: It is not hormones or puberty that causes stress, but it is the relationship. The daughter's distorted view of herself and the unhealthy way she deals with it sets the problem in motion.

Since behavior is easily seen and heart attitudes are not, you may still cling to the theory of hormone-triggered rebellion. If you are, consider these thoughts:

•If hormones caused rebellion, the problem would be universal and measurable in all societies and cultures. The genetic clock would kick in for all children, bringing about rebellion in all adolescents. But it doesn't. Not in any culture does this universally happen, including ours.

•If hormones caused rebellion, how would we explain the healthy families whose teens don't rebel? These kids go through the same hormonal changes but do not seek to overthrow their parents' leadership.

•If hormones caused rebellion, then why isn't medication its cure?

INDEPENDENCE

The From-Parents Theory

A second theory about teen rebellion contends that it is a search for independence. It states that adolescence is the period when children attempt to separate themselves from the parental bonds of love and dependence and move toward an adult identity. In this way, they are "planting their flag," declaring themselves independent and sovereign. As a sign of their independence, teens must develop a different set of values from those of their parents and other authorities. All of this is part of their search for independence, and the tearing away traumatizes relationships.

This theory offers a false sense of comfort to bewildered parents, freeing them from accountability for their teens' behavior. However, it also can discourage parents, causing many to give up before they start. These parents believe that no matter what they do in the early years, conflict is unavoidable. It all adds up to a lose-lose situation for the family.

The independence-rebellion theory is a modern notion that is rooted in the Freudian theory of the personality. According to Freud, the quest to be detached from parental control, from the slavery of a conscience crafted by the parents, is the root cause of teenage rebellion. Thus, to many parents, even Bible-believing ones, rebellion isn't a question of "if," it's a matter of "when." The assumption of the naturalness of rebellion is not, in the final analysis, natural at all. It is simply theory.

Is adolescence really just one continuous, unavoidable struggle filled with endless conflict until independence is achieved? At that point, does the prodigal son or daughter miraculously return home, endearing himself or herself to mom and dad? What part does nurture play? Let's look at this further.

The From-Childhood Reality

In this discussion, we wish we could find a term other than *independence* to use. This is because in popular discussion, the word often carries a connotation of defiance. To be independent basically means to not be dependent. Clearly, man isn't an island and is always dependent in one way or another upon others. In the Christian world and life view, this dependency is both vertical and horizontal. We are forever dependent upon God. "Without Me you can do nothing," Christ said (John 15:5). It is equally true that a believer cannot be all that God intends him to be without the regular and meaningful contributions of other members of the body of Christ (see Romans 12; 1 Corinthians 12; and Ephesians 4). Thus utter independence is not a practical or righteous reality.

Teens do, in a good sense and as part of the maturation process, seek independence. That's a fact of life. But what are they seeking independence from? That question is central to understanding the issues at hand. Through our examination of healthy families, we have found that the quest for independence finds the teen moving away from his childhood and childhood structures, not from relationship with his parents. In strong families, teens *transform* their relationships with their parents, they do not abandon them. Earlier we addressed the "inevitable rebellion" fallacy.

Certainly, sin and its effects permeate everything we are and do. Our bodies, our relationships, our emotions, and our reason are impacted by sin. Thus, we are not so naive as to think that families can avoid problems altogether.

What we *are* saying is that teenage rebellion is not an unavoidable experience. Sin affects marriages as well. Statistically, divorce is very common. However, couples do not and should not see divorce as inevitable. Our God is bigger than that. In the same way, we need not expect the growth from childhood to adulthood to result in a fracturing of the relationship between the teen and parent.

We mentioned that in strong families teens seek to separate themselves from their childhood structures, but what about struggling families? From what are those teens seeking independence? As in the previous example, these teens seek independence from childhood. But this is not the sole issue for them; they also seek independence from unhealthy relationships.

When a fledgling teen is presented with too-strict confinement or no loving boundaries at all, when house rules are required for the kids but not for the parents, when parental hypocrisy causes communication to be less than honest, when the parents' marriage is in a continual state of conflict—then, yes, there is a high probability that the teen will seek to break ties with the family. He or she does so to escape pain, hypocrisy, neglect, or parental dominance, but not because of some preprogrammed genetic time-cue that sends him off in search of independence.

Under these circumstances, parents, as well as childhood associates, are the focus of a child's quest for freedom. The unhealthy aspects of their relationship drive the teen away from his or her parents, just as they would in any relationship. Hence, the teen sets himself or herself against his or her parents, their ideals, and their values. Is this condition reparable? Yes. That is the good news for us Christians. The entire message of God's love is one of reconciliation. In later chapters we will discuss the how-tos of family renewal.

SELF-ESTEEM

The Outside-In Theory

A third rebellion theory considers the role of poor self-esteem in the mix of adolescent conflict. Many believe that a lack of self-esteem is the root cause of teens doing drugs, experiencing academic failure, participating in gang violence, becoming sexually active, and rebelling against their parents.

In America, the issue of self-esteem enhancement can be found everywhere—we read about it, hear about it on the radio, watch it on sitcoms, experience it in the classroom, and tap our feet to its music. Contemporary sociologists, psychologists, and educators alike link healthy self-esteem with happiness, success, physical coordination, and even a child's IQ.

Two sets of words immediately come to mind when defining in contemporary terms what is meant by self-esteem: *self-approval* and *self-validation*. Both are fairly descriptive of what educators are hoping to accomplish with children through self-esteem training. As used in our modern vernacular, *esteem* as a noun means "favorable opinion." *Self-esteem* means "favorable opinion of self."

The idea that children will possess an abiding favorable opinion of self and that this leads to a better life is at the core of America's lust for self-esteem. As self-esteem enhancement gains more significance and legitimacy among the general populace, parenting strategies are continually being adjusted to meet perceived needs. Parents are told to do whatever it takes to make a child feel good about himself or herself, for it is assumed that the possession of right feelings is a necessary step for right behavior.

But is this belief true? Are right personal feelings a necessary prerequisite to right personal behavior? Let's ask the question this way: Do you believe self-esteem causes healthy development in children, or does healthy development produce within children a satisfying sense of self? Which is the stimulus? Which is the response? Might the current method used to manufacture healthy self-esteem be an essential part of the problem?

A Second Opinion

The word *esteem* is used twenty-three times in Scripture, in four different tenses. It is interesting to note that it is never used in reference to loving or approving of oneself. However, it *is* used in reference to considering others. This was Paul's intended meaning when he said, "Let nothing be done through selfish ambition or conceit, but in lowliness of mind let each esteem others better than himself" (Philippians 2:3).

Clearly, a biblical anthropological view of esteem conflicts with conventional secular wisdom. Although their goal is noble, we believe modern self-esteem proponents reverse the equation by insisting that *feeling good* is the precursor to *doing good*. According to that assumption, parents should build healthy self-esteem into their children before requiring anything of them. We take a different approach—in fact, an opposite one. Doing good is the precursor to feeling good. Right behavior leads to right feelings, and the accumulation of right feelings leads to a healthy and biblical view of self.

Here is why we say that: Doing right and consequently feeling right is rooted in a right relationship with God and His Word, and in doing what is required of each of us. When a teen—or a child of any age—lives life in agreement with God's moral mandates, when his or her actions are aligned with God's relational precepts, that teen's conscience bears witness that his or her behavior is in keeping with the ultimate law giver: The Lord of the universe, Jesus Christ. Only when we are rightly aligned with God are we rightly aligned with self.

Between Two Views

Working with parents year after year has given us a better than average opportunity to observe, meet, and respond to moms and dads on both sides of the fence. Regularly we talk to families who are healthy and not so healthy—parents who are managing well and others who are not. If there is one observable fact that stands out above all others, it is the consistency between the two views of self-esteem. Sometimes the obvious is so obvious, it is confusing.

Parents are much more likely to struggle with teenage rebellion if they place a greater emphasis on "self-oriented" self-esteem training in the early years, believing this is the key to all later behavior. That is, parents who place a greater emphasis on how a child feels rather than on how he acts experience a greater percentage of parent-teen conflicts. The degree of conflict appears to be proportional to the amount of early self-orientation emphasized in the home. The fact is, this type of early self-esteem training too often produces dysfunctional children.

In contrast, even a casual survey of healthy parent-teen relationships reveals a completely different conclusion. Self-esteem training among families with the healthiest parent-teen relationships is nearly nonexistent in the early years, and this may actually serve as a source of family humor in the later years. Yet, ironically, children from these homes each have a healthy sense of self.

Parents who instill in their children relationship skills, values, and virtues provide a basis on which a positive sense of self is established. Children emerge from these homes with moral purposefulness, which leads to right behavior, and right behavior leads to a healthy view of self.

It is not right feelings that lead to right behavior, as self-esteem advocates contend. Instead, right behavior which stems from right motives is the genesis of right feelings.

A qualifying word is needed here. We need to set apart the healthy aspects of "self" from the unhealthy ones. We would not want any shadow of doubt cast upon the significance of the following concepts. We must establish a biblical perspective regarding self-respect, self-confidence, self-conviction, personal honor, personal integrity, and personal dignity. The association of these concepts with the word *self* doesn't make them unnecessary or ungodly. These words represent personal ideals that are absolutely necessary for healthy parent-teen relationships.

RELATIONSHIP TRAUMA

The They'll-Make-It Theory

The breakdown of family harmony during the teen years can be attributed to many factors. Mode and style of parenting, a weak marriage, drugs or alcohol abuse, parent manipulation, an over-bearing mother, an absentee father—all will emotionally impact future family relationships. But the most painful relationship setback for children comes with divorce and, as often is the case, subsequent remarriage. As difficult as divorce can be for an adult, it is doubly difficult for children.

Today many believe that divorce and remarriage have a negative impact on children and family relationships. They also contend, though, that children are emotionally resilient and can "bounce back" from the trauma of separated parents.

The Impact Reality

The rate of divorce is so high in the United States that now the family headed by original marriage partners is no longer the statistical norm. Some estimates put this group at slightly more than forty percent of our family population.[1] This means a lot of families with teens are facing the added relationship issues of missing parents and/or the blending of two families. In tackling the impact this has on teen rebellion, we do not intend to condemn anyone's present circumstances. These remarks about divorce are intended to help single parents and blended-family parents understand the source of possible tensions.

From a teen's point of view, divorce violates the unspoken relationship covenant inherent in the family. With divorce comes a sense of betrayal. That betrayal is confirmed in remarriage. Remarriage dashes a child's hope of seeing the family reunited and leaves many children feeling emotionally abandoned. In the vast majority of cases, no child wants to see another man become Dad or another woman become Mom when the biological parent waits in the wings.

The way a child responds to the pain of divorce depends on his or her age. Younger children tend to respond by withdrawing from life, while older children may respond with anger, disappointment, and finally, rejection of relationships. If a child has had a strong attachment to the biological parents, the possibility of teenage stress increases with divorce and remarriage. If the relationship with the stepparent is poor, the probabilities for disaster are even higher.

On the positive side, blended families can avoid rebellion and relational rejection. The factors that make this possible are:

•A strong relationship with the stepparent;

•Confidence that the biological parent is loved;

•Parents who avoid hypocrisy by living out the same values that they require of the teen.

Though both blended and single-parent families have built-in setbacks, God in His grace can help make the best out of every situation.

This brings us to the end of our brief overview of how societal views may have shaped your outlook on the teen years. Now let's take the next step toward restoring and reshaping your relationship with your teen.

QUESTIONS FOR REVIEW

1. Why does the Bible say that rebellion is a heart issue?

2. Write down a thought from the chapter that helped you put the hormone changes of your teen into perspective.

3. Consider each of your teens and indicate what you feel he or she may be seeking independence from.

- Childhood
- Parental dominance
- Pain
- Hypocrisy
- Feeling neglected or unloved

4. List something from your past that contributed to a healthy view of yourself.

5. Do you agree that right behavior leads to right feelings? Why or why not?

CHAPTER THREE

The Myth of Adolescence

Amy needed her mother Ellen's help to get her high school class schedule changed. So the next morning, instead of dropping off her daughter, Ellen parked the car and headed to the office with her. In the hall, Amy whispered, "Please don't walk with me, Mom."

A stab of rejection hit Ellen as her daughter hurried ahead of her. The pain made her want to react even as her mind searched the events of the morning and the night before for the reasons behind her daughter's behavior. She quickened her pace, ready to confront Amy. Just then her daughter turned back and said, "Sorry, Mom. It's just that I feel like a little kid when I walk with you."

IT AIN'T EASY

Amy is caught between two worlds. For eight or nine years, she will no longer be a child, yet she won't be an adult either. She's an *adolescent*—a term derived from a Latin verb meaning "to ripen or grow into maturity." Adolescence is a period of growth when the characteristics of childhood are gradually exchanged for those of adulthood.

There's a difference between the terms *adolescent* and *teen*. The word *teen* (or *teenager*) designates the numerical age span from thirteen to nineteen years, while *adolescent* is a broader term. Adolescence begins with the onset of puberty and ends with physical maturity.

The Bible doesn't use the terms *adolescent, adolescence,* or *teenager,* but refers to children of this approximate age as *youth* or *young men.* For example, Daniel, Shadrach, Meshach, and Abed-Nego were all "young men" when taken to Babylon to serve Nebuchadnezzar (Daniel 1:3–4). Bible scholars place their ages between twelve and fifteen years. David is thought to have been about this same age when he fought Goliath as a "youth" (1 Samuel 17:42).

Regardless of which term is used—*teenager, adolescent, young man,* or *youth*—of those Amy's age, one thing is certain: They're facing the challenge of growing up. But does this mean they have to rebel?

THE CHALLENGE OF ADOLESCENCE

Contrary to popular belief, there are well-adjusted adolescents, as well as not so well-adjusted ones. There are teens with a coherent sense of purpose and others who are desperately seeking one. There are many pro-parent young people around, as well as those whose relationships with their parents are sadly deficient.

The challenge of adolescence isn't new. Socrates, Aristotle, Saint Augustine, and even William Shakespeare spoke of it. As early as 1828, Noah Webster's *American Dictionary of the English Language* defined *adolescence* as the state of growing in the period of life between childhood and manhood. Yet somewhere along the line, public opinion of the teen years switched. No longer are they thought of as challenging. Today they are considered downright bad.

As we close out this century, our society confronts adolescence with a well-established belief that this period is going to be particularly troublesome. As we mentioned in chapter 2, at the turn of the century, G. Stanley Hall wrote what was considered the definitive work on the psychology of adolescence. In his book, *Adolescence,* he concluded that the period was a time of "storm and stress" characterized by teens running the gamut of emotional expressions. His theory became the norm for the next ninety years.[2]

In 1961, James S. Coleman added to that sinking stereotype. His book, *The Adolescent Society,* popularized the theory that peer pressure renders parents voiceless and helpless, unable to cope with the power of peer influence on their teens.[3] Coleman's teenage stereotype has become so ingrained that now, nearly forty years later, good parent-teen relationships are classified as an unexpected outcome. They are often explained away as developmental flukes or family oddities that are impossible to duplicate.

Psychologist Erick Erikson considered adolescence to be a period of "normative crisis."[4] Anna Freud insisted something must be wrong if things went well between parent and teen.[5] Unfortunately, these negative stereotypes have even invaded the church. Pastors and youth pastors often tell struggling parents, "This is to be expected."

More than ever, parents today are demoralized by clichés, slogans, and negative public examples. There is no conspiracy on the part of public voices to demoralize an entire generation of new parents, but that is exactly what is happening. Not only are young parents deeply discouraged by the clichés and negative slogans, but the resulting defeatist attitudes often lead to self-fulfilling conclusions. Years ago we heard a pastor say, "You get what you honor." Often we have seen that premise played out in the context of parenting. When parents assume their child is bad, they then "find" badness everywhere. Preconceptions have remarkable power. As parents, we cannot allow ourselves to slip into a mind-set that expects our children to be and do wrong.

Unfortunately, the teen myth has created parental despair and apathy. It has also robbed positive parenting of its credibility. Like the normal-birthed Mundugumor tribe member who sees his or her artistic ability but discredits it, young parents are skeptical when they hear the occasional voice saying, "I really enjoy my teenagers." Automatically when they hear a parent talk about their terrific teens, they think, *Yes, but what aren't you telling us?*

In spite of these prevailing predictions, you can have a great relationship with your teens. Parents are always in a position to make a difference. The fact is, *you are in the process of making a difference right now.*

God ordained that you, the parent, serve as the primary shaper of your child's heart and mind. This is not a job to be taken up grudgingly or with hesitation. God will provide all the wisdom and discernment you need. Certainly there will be difficult days to endure, confusing times to pray through, failures to rise up from, paths to straighten, and mountains to climb. But at the end of the day, you are the most powerful influence on your child's life. God has made it so, and He will see you through to the very end.

THE MYTH OF ADOLESCENCE

Some people have taken the myth of inevitable rebellion and turned it into a cause and effect. They say the transition years between childhood and adulthood are artificial, created by industrialization. In a nonindustrial society, kids become adults overnight. Therefore, our children's abnormal delay in growing up causes rebellion. This is commonly referred to as the *myth of adolescence.*

Only a small number of the clinical population holds this view, but bits and pieces of it have filtered down to parents.

Though few are aware of the myth's origin, the cause-and-effect relationship of adolescence and rebellion seems plausible. But is it?

The myth about the myth presupposes that the modern-day maturing process—that is, the extended phase of adolescence needed to prepare our children to enter the working adult community—must be bad in some way since it causes rebellion. But this view raises some perplexing questions about the nature of maturity. Does your child become an adult when he matures, or does he mature when he becomes an adult? What is maturity, anyway? What is adulthood?

FROM CRAYONS TO CARS

When Hal clasped his son's tuxedoed shoulder and wished him a good time at the prom, he couldn't help noticing that the boy he'd held in his lap now had hard muscles and stood eye-to-eye with him. Yet he also couldn't help saying, "Drive safely." Instinctively, Hal knew the physical maturity of his son did not ensure social and moral maturity. Neither was it a sign of legal maturity.

Growing up has more than one aspect to it. Before we can put the challenge of adolescence into perspective, we first must look at the four classes of maturity: legal, physical, social/intellectual, and moral. How you view these four levels of maturity highly influences how you view adolescence in general.

LEGAL MATURITY

Legal maturity is defined by statute or by custom, not by experience. Every group of people in the world follows some generally accepted guideline which marks a child's rite of passage into adulthood. This is typically a rather formal definition and marks the child's inclusion into the adult community with all its rights and responsibilities.

For example, in America most states allow a sixteen-year-old the legal right to drive a car. But that same sixteen-year-old cannot legally vote until he is eighteen. He can legally play the California lottery as an eighteen-year-old, but he cannot legally buy alcoholic beverages until he is twenty-one.

Of course, the mere passage of time does not signal maturity at all levels. Like Hal in the foregoing example, we know that having achieved "legal age" does not necessarily indicate that a teen is emotionally, socially, financially, or spiritually an adult. Yet in a legal sense, the child is now an adult.

PHYSICAL MATURITY

All humans of every tongue, tribe, and nation have the same patterns of physical growth and development. As a result, every person reaches physical maturity at approximately the same time.

Physical growth is rapid during infancy and early childhood then slows just before puberty. A spurt of rapid growth follows puberty and extends into mid-adolescence; then it plateaus and slows down until adulthood.

Between eighteen and twenty years of age, the skeletal-growth process ends. This is marked by two events: the achievement of maximum body growth (height) and ossification of the sacral bones. Physical maturity, then, is marked both by the attainment of maximum growth and the cessation of growth.

SOCIAL/INTELLECTUAL MATURITY

The definition of legal adulthood is fairly objective. A child reaches a prescribed age assigned by the society, and he is declared "legally of age." Physical maturity also can be objectively observed. In contrast, social/intellectual maturity has no such benchmark and is highly influenced by each society.

To explain this class of maturity, we'll begin by defining the terms *social maturity* and *intellectual maturity*. *Social maturity* refers to one's readiness to be an active participant in social policy and in contributing to the good of the society at large. *Intellectual maturity* speaks to the minimum level of intellectual and academic attainment necessary to function in the adult community. From those two definitions, it can be said that the level of social/intellectual maturity required before one can enter the adult community is determined by the simplicity or complexity of each society.

Every society sets its own minimum social/intellectual standard that must be met before a person is accepted as an adult. This basic law establishes the length of adolescence within every society. As parents, we can gain important insights by taking a look at this basic law in four different cultural settings: primitive/tribal, pre- and mid-industrial America, post-modern America, and first-century Judaism.

PRIMITIVE/TRIBAL SOCIETIES

Margaret Meade, a noted anthropologist who worked with primitive tribes, showed that in primitive tribal societies children can pass directly from childhood into adulthood without going through an adolescent phase. This happens because preparation for adulthood in such settings presents few of the social, intellectual, or moral challenges that are common to advanced societies. We have personally witnessed the social/intellectual phenomenon in primitive settings. Many of the skills needed to participate in the adult community—fishing, hunting and planting, for example—are actually gained before the onset of puberty.

Primitive simplicity does not move children into adulthood earlier, but brings adult status closer in age to childhood. This last point is further demonstrated by examining adolescence in pre-industrial America.

PRE- AND MIDINDUSTRIAL AMERICA

The social and intellectual skills needed to participate as an adult in America a hundred years ago were far less demanding than they are today. At the turn of the twentieth century, it was not uncommon for girls and boys to marry at fourteen or fifteen years of age and to set up housekeeping.

A simpler life meant a simpler transition into adulthood and a shorter period of adolescence. This does not mean that children back then matured sooner; rather, what was required for social and intellectual maturity was far less demanding than it is today.

POSTMODERN AMERICA

The phrase *postmodern America* is a relatively new societal classification that marks another level of social/intellectual advancement. Today, we live in the Age of Information. This term describes the volumes of current knowledge available to the average citizen. Both the volume and complexity of new information highly influences the length of adolescence in our day.

We live in an age of microchip technology. We talk of cyberspace, virtual reality, fiber optics, web sites, multi-tasking, and gigabytes. Adulthood in America, as well as in our European and Asian industrialized counterparts, requires the attainment of a variety of sophisticated skills and abilities unimagined just fifty years ago. The very complexity of American adult life evokes a type of moratorium on early entry into adulthood. That's why a period of adolescent ripening is absolutely necessary in our current day. There is simply too much to learn.

Society does not have confidence to allow a fifteen-year-old to drive a bus, fly a commercial airliner, undertake the rigors of an emergency room doctor or public school teacher, compete in the bond market, design bridges, build skyscrapers, or handle a thousand other intellectually demanding and skill-intensive jobs.

The intricacies of modern adulthood will not allow teenagers to participate on an equal footing with adults. Adolescents lack a type of wisdom and judgment that is gained through time with age and experience. The period of adolescence in postmodern America is necessary to better prepare our teens to compete effectively as adults in our society and world.

FIRST-CENTURY JUDAISM

The "youth" phase in historical Judaism linked childhood with adulthood. It was a secondary phase very similar to the adolescent phase found in pre-industrial America. In biblical times, maturity was not synonymous with adulthood. That distinction is important to grasp.

A minor reached "maturity" at thirteen, but adulthood came later, usually at around eighteen to twenty years of age. Maturity in the Hebrew culture spoke of a mixture of certain legal rights and moral obligations. It was a time when a child entered the adult world as a participant in religious and social ceremonies.

The Jewish bar mitzvah (which refers to the time when one becomes a son of the Mosaic law) served this purpose for boys. It marked the beginning of a youth's independent legal status and the age of moral responsibility. At this point, a youth became a moral equal with his parents. He could legally buy and trade in the marketplace, be a witness in court, even be married; but he was not "adult enough" to sell inherited real estate (the minimum age for such matters was eighteen), nor could he be a judge until he was twenty-one.[6]

In the Bible God defines adulthood in Numbers 14:29. This Old Testament passage is the only narrative in Scripture that refers to the age of adult accountability. You may remember that God declared those twenty years of age and older (except for Caleb and Joshua) would die in the wilderness for their sin of unbelief. The punishment was pronounced on the "adult popu-lation."

An examination of social/intellectual maturity in four differ-ent cultural settings makes one thing clear: The parameters of adolescence are governed by the adult demands of the culture in which an individual lives. The simpler the society, the sooner a child moves into adulthood. The more complex it is, the longer the adolescent transition. This is true of our society. That is why we believe that the period of adolescence is not a myth, but a nec-essary reality.

MORAL MATURITY

It is natural to think that moral maturity follows the same growth patterns as does physical or social/intellectual maturity. Since a child tends to mature in each of these categories just before entrance to adulthood, many assume that personal morality fol-lows suit. Not so. Such thinking actually delays moral maturity by removing from parents a sense of urgency. Childhood is the period for imparting moral instruction and directing moral training, but please note that adolescence is when principles of right living, thinking, and acting should be realized. In a biblical context, moral maturity (thinking and acting in harmony with God's moral law) should show itself between the ages of thirteen and fifteen.

By the time children reach the teen years, they should have begun acquiring a moral code to which they adhere with increas-ing frequency. Adherence is dependent upon three things: moral knowledge (what does God's moral law say?), moral reason (what does the law mean?), and parental example (how valid is the law in the life of those insisting on it?). Moral maturity means your teen not only knows right from wrong, he or she knows *why* right is right and wrong is wrong.

If these three steps can be achieved in your home, a great

family experience will be yours. Why? Because the greatest influence on relationships are the values of the heart. Common values unify; conflicting values war against intimate healthy relationships, especially in the teen years.

The Benefits of Moral Training

1. Moral training established during the preschool and elementary school years is the basis of self-assurance and relational success during the teen years.

2. Moral health is the foundation upon which emotional, intellectual, and creative ventures flourish.

3. The child who appropriates moral wisdom has the best chance of being a happy, well-adjusted, and successful adult (Proverbs 3:13–18).

4. Moral health is the armor that protects kids from drugs, alcohol, unhealthy habits, and delinquency.

5. Moral health is related to high motivation and drive for achievement—in school, work, and play.

6. Children with high moral standards have deeper relationships and more honest friends.

7. Morally trained children are less likely to succumb to peer pressure, more open to constructive criticism, and better informed.

8. Morally healthy children have closer relationships with their siblings, parents, and grandparents.

9. Morally mature teens are appreciated by those outside the family—teachers, coaches, and employers.

10. Moral health is the basis for family health.

You want your teen to be your moral equal long before he or she reaches adulthood physically, socially, or intellectually. The decision to be honest is the same whether a teen makes it during a geometry test or an adult makes it when turning in an expense report. The fact that adults and teens are both on the same page morally forms the basis of *Reaching the Heart of Your Teen*. We will cover this further in part 2.

But before we do, let's deal with the most obvious questions. What about the teen who's lagging behind morally? What if a teen has no desire to conform to family standards and values? What if the parents are willing to change but the teen is not? What if the teen is willing to change but the parent is not? Is there any hope for this family? Yes, absolutely. A values-based approach to parenting and family life is more powerful than present circumstances. It will take work, and relational healing for some. But the outcome can be glorious.

QUESTIONS FOR REVIEW

1. After having read this chapter, how would you define the word *adolescent* to a friend?

2. Up until now, what has been your attitude toward your child's teen years? Have you feared or expected rebellion?

3. When you thought of your children maturing, was there an aspect you did not consider (legal, physical, social/intellectual, moral)? If so, why?

4. When you first read Numbers 14:29 (either in the past or in the context of this book), what was your response to God's sparing all under the age of twenty?

5. Do you have any trouble accepting that morally you are on the same footing as your teen? Why or why not?

CHAPTER FOUR

The Power of Relationship

As we travel from city to city, leading parenting conferences, it seems that the only things on our itinerary that change are the names and faces of hurting parents. Feeling confused and betrayed, they share a common story. "We don't understand! Bobby was raised in the Church from the time he was born. We sent him to a Christian school. He participated in all the youth programs. But now as a teenager, he has rejected our values. Why?"

What would cause a teen to reject the values taught him in early life? There are many answers to this question, but at the top of the list is something the Bible calls *depravity*. Man knows what is right, but still he chooses to go his own way. The apostle Paul saw many people defecting from the faith and listed some of the reasons people drift away from God: fear (2 Timothy 1:7), loneliness (2 Timothy 4:16), greed (1 Timothy 6:9–10), immorality (1 Timothy 5:11–12), and legalism (1 Timothy 4:3–4). These may be the same reasons teens drift away from their parents and their values.

There are other factors that may lead teens to abandon the security of their parents' love. We live in a society that is fundamentally hostile toward the family. Concerned parents who want to raise good children are virtually at war with the community. This was not always the case. Fifty years ago a shared Judeo-Christian ethic produced a social harmony and unity that we no longer experience today. At that time, even bad parents could raise good children because the society had safety nets in place to pick up the slack when moms and dads failed. If a teen had a negligent parent during the 1950s, neighbors, teachers, Little League coaches, and the community at large provided the moral direction the child was lacking. This happened because communities operated from one set of values. All values had common meaning; nothing was relative.

Today we live in a society that believes that *morals* are relative. As a result, communities sharing common moral standards are virtually nonexistent. That is why today you can be a good parent and still turn out a wayward child. Without a moral community surrounding and upholding your values, you must fight alone against television, pornography, drugs, premarital sex, crude public advertising, values-based education, degrading schools, and negative peer pressure. Parents can get really depressed when listing the moral differences between their homes and their communities.

Still, there is a parent factor to consider in confronting teenage rebellion. The period of adolescence is the culmination of all that has gone on before in a child's life. All interaction between parent and child in the formative years—right or wrong, the result of intent or neglect—strongly shapes the social and relational characteristics of the child before he or she becomes a teen. This can be a frightening thought for parents. Realization that the thread of adolescent behavior is tied either to adequate or faulty training in early childhood (and in many cases, if no correction or encouragement comes, will extend into adulthood) is a sobering thought, to say the least.

Having stated that, we wish to move forward. As far as we are concerned, there is no need to bring up what was done wrong in the past. We have all made similar mistakes. That was yesterday, and today is a new day. We all need a fresh start. Thankfully, our God is the God of new beginnings. The problems you may be facing may be the result of sin on the part of you, your teen, your community, or a combination of all three. Regardless of the source of rebellious influences, the starting point for renewal and healing will always be the same—your relationship with your teen.

REBEL WITH A CAUSE

When Mike and Patty went to counseling with their daughter Megan, they thought the issues were schoolwork, choice of friends, and broken family rules. After a few preliminary sessions of airing grievances, the counselor began to ask "why" questions. Time after time, Megan shrugged and answered, "I don't know."

Mike and Patty stepped in, suggesting possible reasons for Megan's behavior. "She grew so fast and always looked older than her age. She's not like our other daughter; Megan's always had an independent streak."

In the middle of her parents' speculation, Megan burst out, "What do you expect? Chrissy has always been your favorite. I was always the 'big girl,' the one who was to blame...."

Their daughter's revelation stunned Mike and Patty. They loved both girls. For the rest of the day, their minds ran reruns of the past. In bed that night, they talked. And as they thought back upon their behavior, the truth became clear. Somehow in their delight with their mild-tempered, golden-haired second daughter, they'd neglected their older one.

Unfortunately, this scenario is all too common. Each time a parent comes to us with such a story, we ask, "What came first?" Was Megan's continued defiance the cause of her poor relationship with her mom and dad? Or did an unintentional but nevertheless weakened relationship frustrate Megan to the point of noncompliance and rebellion?

Although rebellion is basic to man's nature and the root cause of many human conflicts, we have discovered that rebellion itself on the part of teens is not necessarily the root cause of all parent-teen crises. Many times it's not rules that teens rebel against; it's the people who set the rules. Working with teens in conflict with their parents has taught us this truth: When a teen is known and characterized by ongoing rebellion, the root problem is usually as much relational as it is moral.

Ouch! We know that statement can hurt. And we realize there may be many catalysts to rejecting a relationship. A physically or emotionally absent father, an overbearing mother, drugs, alcohol, physical or emotional abuse, not enough or too many rules, an under-controlled or over-controlled child, divorce, remarriage—all of these factors can produce stress. Whatever the cause, however, the object of rejection is always the same—the relationship with parents. Why? Because that's where pain is felt. The striving for independence, confused search for identity, frightening influence of peers, anger and battles of wills, yelling, screaming, and threats—all these are symptoms, but not the cause. For teens characterized by rebellion, they're conclusions, not starting points. If you want to fix the problem, start at the foundation—work on your relationship.

PARENTS WITHOUT A CLUE

When Mike and Patty realized they'd neglected to build a strong relationship with Megan, they wept and asked God to forgive them. The next day they faced their daughters, unsure of how to fix the problem, of how to remain the parents without repeating old mistakes. It was time for Mike and Patty to make a new start with their kids, but they didn't know how. Perhaps you're asking the same question they asked: What does making a new start look like?

First of all, seeking to rebuild parent-teen relationships does not mean abdicating your role or responsibilities as a parent, nor does it mean you should let your teen go wherever his or her passions lead. Adolescence is a time when your son or daughter is best served when you lead by your influence and strength of relationship, rather than by the power of your authority. The truth is, once your kids hit the teen years, your relationship—good or bad—is the greatest asset or liability you have.

Our comments here are not intended to minimize the significance of sinful patterns of either teen or parent. However, we do want to speak directly to the power of right or wrong relationships, which often foster or discourage sinful conflict. Relationship-building is the key to successful teen parenting, but this takes time. There are no shortcuts to building new relationships or mending old ones. This takes effort, and there may be some pain involved.

Pain! Our society doesn't like pain. We want it to go away—now! In our efforts to relieve ourselves of misery, too often we look for temporary solutions that mask the problem but will not fix it. Gary's older brother suffered almost daily from terrible migraine headaches. His only relief was two aspirin and the hope of sleep. Once during a routine dental checkup, the dentist noticed that one of his crooked incisors was placing abnormal pressure on his upper jaw. A decision was made to remove the tooth for the benefit of the jaw. This turned out to be a right decision, although not for the reason it was made—for after the tooth was removed, our brother's migraines disappeared. Months later the doctors concluded that a pressure-packed tooth had been the source of all his pain. Fixing the problem at the source relieved him of his misery.

Parents struggling with teens too often look for medicine that will mask the problems temporarily rather than get to the root cause. Often we want to fix the child, the youth group, the school, or a particular circumstance. But none of those "solutions" will fix the problem.

We are suggesting an alternative approach. We believe that when we stop trying to improve our teens by controlling them or their circumstances and instead focus on improving our relationship with them, two things happen. First, we put the focus where it belongs—on relationship. Second, we start to parent by our influence rather than by our authority.

LEAD, DON'T PUSH

When you have teenagers, it's important to lead by your influence rather than push by your authority. We can demonstrate this principle by using a common shoelace. Stretch one out on a flat surface in front of you. Consider the end nearer you the bottom and the other end farther away the top. Now put your finger at the bottom of the shoelace and begin pushing. What happens? The shoelace begins to stack up in loops and tangles as you push, but it does not move forward. In fact, the more you push, the more it twists and turns, moving in every direction but the one in which you want it to go. Now take the other end of the shoelace and begin pulling. What happens? You can lead the shoelace in any direction.

A values-based parenting approach teaches moms and dads how to lead in such a way that their teens desire to follow. Many parents wish to move their parent-teen relationship from where it is to where it should be, but they find resistance because they are pushing from the bottom rather than leading from the top. They are attempting to force change by the power of their authority, instead of leading by the power of their influence.

AUTHORITY AND INFLUENCE.

Managing or mismanaging these two factors will make all the difference as to how peaceful or turbulant the teen years will be for your family. We will devote the rest of this chapter to developing a proper understanding of how to correctly use your authority with your teens. Later we will discuss how you can help your child internalize values; this is the key that allows you to lead by your influence. But first, let's talk about your authority—more specifically, how *not* to abuse it.

Authority has always been a struggle for humankind. From birth, children struggle with it and as we grow older it doesn't get

---

COMMON TRAITS OF STRONG FAMILIES

1. A core of shared values that all members embrace.
2. Ability to communicate with each other.
3. Parents who are not afraid to say "I was wrong."
4. Teens who are willing to accept "No" for an answer.
5. Parents who are approachable about their own sin.
6. The marriage as a recognized priority for family health.
7. Family members who make time to be with each other and to attend each other's events.
8. Parents who are not afraid of the teen years.
9. Teens who are confident of their parents' trust in them.
10. Family members who are loyal to each other.
11. lanned family events.
12. Elevation of conflict resolution above conflict avoidance.
13. A corporate sense of responsibility to all members.
14. Family rules swapped for family courtesies as the teen gets older and matures.
15. Acceptance of the premise that the family unit is more important than the individual.

any easier. Some people can't seem to live with it; most of us understand that you can't live harmoniously without it.

In the Christian family, the Bible not only provides the basis of all authority, but also the ethics governing the exercise of authority. Biblical authority is beautiful because it is morally focused. Similar to the character of love (1 Corinthians 13:5–7) biblical authority is not presumptous, proud, unkind, or unfair; instead, it is gentle, consistent, gracious, and full of integrity. It's motivated by love and used only when needed. It's purpose is to guide by encouragement and restraint. Authority is necessary because law and order for the family and society are dependent on its proper administration. But authority can be taken to the extreme. Too much authority leads to totalitarianism, insufficient authority leads to injustice and social choas, this is true for nations and true for families.

In societal settings, whether it be a nation of families or a single family, the amount of rules, regulations and authority needed to govern a people is a reflection of the moral consensus of the people. Moral consensus refers to values mutually agreed upon that govern individual behavior for the common good. The more values we share in common as a community of people, the less there is a need for coercive government to bring social order. In contrast, the more individual values conflict with societal values the more intrusive government must become to insure social harmony. That same law of social order applies to our families.

What we are striving for in our homes is social order and unity without coercive authority, especially when there is a teenager living in the house. In order to achieve that end, we must balance the need for parental authority with our teen's growing sense of personal responsibility. The closer the family draws morally, the less there is a need for rulership by authority. Figure 1 on the next page demonstrates this truth.

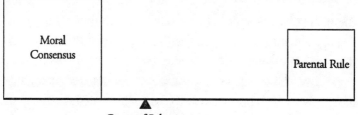

Center of Balance

figure 1

Please note the greater the moral consensus among family members, the less the need for parental rule.

Figure 2 demonstrates the opposite effect. The less the moral consensus (that is, the greater the moral disparity between parent and teen), the more parental control must increase in order to maintain the balance of social order within the family. During the teen years, whenever you increase parental controls you increase the likelihood of teen conflict.

Please note that the center of balance has been redefined in figure 2. It has shifted toward more control to compensate for less moral unity. As we will learn in a moment, this is where all parents start out with their children, but it is not where we should be once our kids become teens.

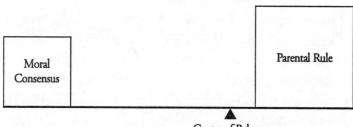

Center of Balance

figure 2

ESTABLISHING MORAL COMMON GROUND

The belief that commonly held values leads to unity is not new. The apostle Paul encouraged the Philippians with these words: "Therefore if there is any consolation in Christ, if any comfort of love, if any fellowship of the Spirit, if any affection and mercy, fulfill my joy by being like-minded, having the same love, being of one accord, of one mind" (Philippians 2:1–2). Being like-minded, having the same love, and being of one accord—these attributes represent a noble goal for a Christian family. But how is such a goal attained? Only by establishing moral common ground.

In the family, just as in the Body of Christ, whenever there is a breakdown in relationships, that failure ultimately is tied to a breakdown in values. Because of that, you cannot start to build or rebuild strong relational bridges without a moral consensus. When Bible-based, it is common values that strengthen family ties. They are the glue that holds families together.

A moral consensus formed by common values also involves moral reciprocity. By this we mean that the moral rules for the teen are observed equally by the parents. When you remove the possibility of a double standard ("Do as I say, not as I do"), you remove the likelihood of hypocrisy. In its place will be relational security, confidence, believability, trustworthiness, partnership, family unity, and thus, harmony.

We want you to think positively about the future. We want you to enjoy your *adolescent adult.* Adolescent adult? How can a teenager be both an adolescent and an adult? This is an important concept to grasp, because a principal factor in successful teen parenting is having an adult relationship with your teenage son or daughter, even though he or she isn't an adult physically, socially, or intellectually. An adolescent adult is a teen who can relate morally on par with adults. He possesses the moral graces in both conversation and action. This can only happen when your teen achieves moral maturity. When that is reached, you the parent will also enjoy the benefits of moral consensus. You can start leading more by the strength of your relationship and less by the power of your authority.

THE AUTHORITY EXCHANGE

Are you using more or less of your authority now that your children are in the teen years? We hope it's less. As children move into adolescence, the need for parental rule should decline in proportion to the child's increased rate of moral self-rule. The word *moral* in the previous sentence is operative.

The ontological fact that children are born with a natural propensity for selfish self-rule dates back to Cain and Abel. Children are born self-oriented; biblical ethics are other-oriented. The tension between the two creates conflict that must be resolved by parental leadership. The duty of parents is to redirect a child's wayward tendencies toward behavior that is pleasing to the Lord. This is done by encouraging right attitudes and actions while discouraging wrong ones. To encourage and discourage such behavior, parents need to exercise their authority.

By their authority, parents direct their children to virtuous behavior, reinforcing compliance by extrinsic means until the child has the moral maturity to govern himself by intrinsic values. This assumes a decreasing emphasis on leadership by authority and an increasing emphasis on leadership by influence. We can further demonstrate this point by looking at various phases of development.

Let's start with infancy. Infancy is the zenith of parental authority. This is when all of life's decisions are made by mom and dad. The child's parents determine when he or she will eat, sleep, stay awake, have a bath, play on the blanket, or go for a stroller ride. Such tight supervision is absolutely necessary at this age, since the child simply does not have the moral conscience or intellect to know what is best and what is needed.

Now consider parental authority in the life of a five-year-old. By the age of five, a child has gained some internal mastery over his life and actions. That mastery allows him a degree of corresponding freedom. The decreased need of parental authority is proportionate to the increased amounts of age-appropriate, self-imposing controls. Please note that parental authority does not decrease; only the need for its use diminishes.

For example, there are some activities in a five-year-old's life that no longer need mom or dad's direct approval. A five-year-old can come and go from the backyard, pick out a board game, go to his or her room, put together a puzzle, or play with the family hamster. While there is a gate preventing his or her one-year-old brother access to the upstairs bedroom, the five-year-old navigates the barrier without need of parental approval. Why? Because such approval is assumed. Once the child continually demonstrates responsible behavior in these areas, parental policing is not necessary. Our point is this: Although parental authority is still a considerable influence in a five-year-old's life, it is not as sweeping in its control as it was a few years earlier.

How about the child at age ten? Because of his or her increased ability to sustain periods of healthy self-rule, the need for visible authority is substantially reduced. A ten-year-old should be rapidly approaching moral maturity. Again, it is not that mom and dad's authority is no longer valid—it is only that the need for external control is diminishing. Gradually, parental control is being replaced by parental influence, and extrinsic motivation governing the child's life is being replaced by intrinsic beliefs ruling from his or her heart.

Now we come to the teen years—the time you should be striving for moral consensus through moral maturity. Internalized virtues of the heart, not parental authority, should be ruling. Possessing moral maturity does not mean your teen is spiritually all-knowing, but it does mean he or she knows and lives the otherness standards of Scripture. Moral maturity connects parents and teens at the heart with common character traits and mutual respect and honor. At the same time, both maintain the uniqueness of their God-given relationship as parents and child.

We'd like to offer just one final point of clarification. When we speak of leading by your influence, not your authority, we want to be clear that we are not suggesting that you eliminate house or family rules. Our teens are still accountable to us, and there are community tasks and responsibilities that need to be maintained. Teens must complete their chores, make their own beds, clean up after themselves, be home at a reasonable hour, and, yes, comply with parental instruction. What we are saying is that the basic tasks of life should take on new meaning—a moral one—in response to a relationship with the family and not simply a response to some cold and impersonal set of rules.

Parental authority should not disappear during the teen years, but it should be used as a backup to enforce times of non-compliance. That is how government works in a free society. The majority of your leadership, and your teen's response to it, should be based on a new level of cooperation that calls everyone to live responsibly within the confines of the community called "family."

Please understand, our children will always be our children, and we will always be their parents. But sooner or later they will grow into moral maturity, no longer requiring parental policing of their behavior. What we are advocating is: the sooner the better.

QUESTIONS FOR REVIEW

1. Think through the statement "Teens rebel against relation-ships." Do you agree or disagree? Why or why not?

2. What has been the focus of your parenting to this point?

3. The "moral-relational" model of parenting was mentioned frequently in this chapter. Give a definition of it in your own words.

4. Does your family have some common ground? If so, what is it?

5. What role do strong morals play in your emotional stability?

PART II

REACHING

the

HEART

of your

TEEN

The Key to Moral Maturity

We start this chapter with two truths. The first is that parenting is a process leading to maturity. Who among us was mature enough to have children *before* our children came? It seems that children are not just a blessing that results from marriage—they are part of the process that produces two mature beings: mom and dad. The second truth is that nothing of value comes quickly. Whether you're just starting to build a strong family or beginning to repair a weakened one, the process takes time.

If we have learned two things from counseling parents at war with their teens, they are: It is natural to try to control something that is out of control, and change can be frightening, especially for parents. Yet we are asking you to face this fear, to put aside your authority, and to begin to work toward leading your teen by the influence of your relationship.

One father told us, "If I give up my authority, my kid will run all over me." Another mom explained, "Lead by my influence? I don't have any influence over my daughter. She does what she pleases. I can't stop her." These are very real concerns. But if they are legitimate, then it's time you consider a new alternative. Apparently controlling by your authority hasn't worked for you. But something else can.

THE STRATEGY

Several years ago, Gary had to have a root canal. For some, just the thought of the procedure can bring back painful memories. But this episode wasn't too bad. In fact, it was rather tolerable. Much of the credit goes to the dentist, who took a few minutes before the surgery to walk Gary through the entire process. He explained the problem, showed him diagrams, then told him how the procedure was done and what had to be accomplished in the first session. He even told Gary when he might feel some discomfort or hear some crunching. Because the dentist took the time to outline his strategy, Gary felt more comfortable. Knowing where the doctor was taking him gave him more confidence, both in the man's professional skills and in the actual procedure.

What that dentist did for Gary, we want to do for you. We're going to do something we wish other authors would do. We're going to give you the strategy for the rest of our book right here, right now. We want you to know where you're headed and how we plan to get you there. Let's look at the rest of our journey chapter by chapter.

Chapter Five

In the pages that follow, we will encourage you to consider a better way to lead your teens. Instead of using *more* of your authority, you will learn the benefits of using less and leading instead by the power of your influence. The key is to help your child internalize values. We will clearly explain the process of helping your children of all ages internalize values and make them their own. Once the values are in their hearts, you will be leading by your influence.

Chapter Six

Next, we will explore the subject of starting over. Practically speaking, where do you begin? This chapter offers practical suggestions on how to rebuild credibility with a teenager who doesn't believe you care. Everything from this chapter can be applied immediately...and the ideas work.

Chapter Seven

This chapter contrasts two popular family structures: *interdependent* and *independent*. Your teen's sense of identity and belonging will be either encouraged or discouraged by his or her perception of the family. The closer you are to the interdependent family model, the greater your influence will be in contrast to that of your teen's peers.

Chapter Eight

It is here that we will begin to discuss communication. This chapter introduces five ways to say "I love you" to your kids. These are emotional love languages that can help you reach your teen's heart and satisfy his or her need to know that you really do care. We all desire to communicate love to our children, but often even our best efforts may seem to go unnoticed or unappreciated. Learning how to say "I love you" in your teen's emotional love language can make all the difference in your relationship.

Chapter Nine

This chapter continues our discussion on communication. We surveyed one hundred teenagers in the ninth through twelfth grades, asking them to list the reasons some teens don't listen or talk to their parents in a meaningful way. The results are enlightening and force all of us to evaluate how we listen and speak to our kids.

Chapter Ten

We conclude our thoughts on communication with basic guidelines for good communication. Do you know how to talk to your kids so they will listen and how to listen in a way that will cause your kids to talk? Good communication methods are crucial to the rebuilding process and necessary to maintain healthy families.

Chapter Eleven

The fact that you are now leading by your influence does not mean that you will no longer be giving instructions that call for compliance. Do you know how to give instructions in such a way that will not frustrate you or your teen, but will cause him or her to do what is asked? This chapter will tell you how.

Chapters Twelve and Thirteen

These chapters deal with the encouragement of right behavior and the correction of wrong behavior. What is the most effective way to discipline a teenager? Should you punish him or her? Do you know when a verbal reminder is adequate and when the full weight of justice is called for? These chapters deal with the many aspects of correcting a teen's wayward behavior.

Chapter Fourteen

In our final chapter we will challenge you and your teen in your new relationship. You will learn how to view your new relationship with your kids from a heavenly perspective and discover how to keep that perspective alive.

Now that you know where we are going, let's get started by asking the question "What is morality?"

WHAT IS MORALITY?

Today morality comes in all shapes and sizes. "If it feels right, do it" says one bumper sticker. Even in Christian homes values differ. There's a tendency to end up with a potluck of morality—

some from our folks, some from Bible teachers and book writers, some from society's subtle influence.

BIBLICAL ONE ANOTHERS

• *Do not steal. Do not lie. Do not deceive one another.*—Leviticus 19:11 (NIV)

• This is what the LORD Almighty says: "Administer true justice; *show mercy and compassion to one another.*"—Zechariah 7:9 (NIV)

• "A new command I give you: *Love one another.* As I have loved you, so you must love one another."—John 13:34 (NIV)

• *Be devoted to one another* in brotherly love. *Honor one another* above yourselves.—Romans 12:10 (NIV)

• *Be of the same mind toward one another;* do not be haughty in mind, but associate with the lowly. Do not be wise in your own estimation.—Romans 12:16 (NAS)

• *Accept one another,* then, just as Christ accepted you, in order to bring praise to God.—Romans 15:7 (NIV)

• You, my brothers, were called to be free. But do not use your freedom to indulge the sinful nature; rather, *serve one another in love.*—Galatians 5:13 (NIV)

• Be completely humble and gentle; be patient *bearing with one another* in love.—Ephesians 4:2 (NIV)

• And *be kind to one another,* tenderhearted, *forgiving one another,* just as God in Christ forgave you.—Ephesians 4:32 (NKJ)

• *Submitting yourselves one to another* in the fear of God.—Ephesians 5:21 (KJV)

• Let the word of Christ richly dwell within you, with all wisdom *teaching and admonishing one another* with psalms and hymns and spiritual songs, singing with thankfulness in your hearts to God.—Colossians 3:16 (NAS)

• Therefore *encourage one another* and *build each other up.*—1 Thessalonians 5:11 (NIV)

• Let us consider how to *stimulate one another to love and good deeds.*—Hebrews 10:24 (NAS)

• *Offer hospitality to one another* without grumbling.—1 Peter 4:9 (NIV)

What's so wrong with taking a potluck approach? Why do parents need to test their values against the standard of God's Word? First and foremost, Christian values reflect the person of

Christ. Such values trigger a child's consciousness of God and eternity. The natural world is seen, heard, felt, smelled, and tasted. But the supernatural world is revealed through quiet and unseen things such as revelation by the Holy Spirit, faith, and the values that reflect both.

Second, because biblical values are others-oriented, a child trained in them is bathed in otherness sensitivity—a prerequisite for healthy and enduring relationships. Jesus was others-oriented and set the ethical standard for the "one another" of Scripture. Biblical values produce the moral mandate of Scripture that requires a love-God, love-your-neighbor sensitivity (Mark 12:28–31). I should not base my conduct toward you on how valuable you are to me nor on any value found in our humanity, but on how beloved we are to God (Romans 8:35–39).

Third, biblical values promote unity. Moral relativism segregates society into cultural subgroups, but biblical values are socially, racially, ethnically, economically, and educationally blind (Galatians 3:28; Colossians 3:11; and James 2:1–10). Without God's morality, behavior is governed by personal preference.

MORE THAN THE MIND

Godly values instilled into a person's life will make a positive difference whether that person acknowledges God or not. But it is the hope and focus of Christian parents to raise a morally responsible person who realizes that Jesus Christ belongs in his or her life. Only then does moral training go beyond the mind and into the heart. Only then do God's values go beyond being a positive life influence to being a way of life.

Does your son or daughter know Jesus Christ? Pray, pray, pray that he or she does, but don't let your desire blind you. Unless your teen's life reflects a profession of faith made as a young child, leave room for the possibility that your teen hasn't really put his or her faith in Jesus. Moral common ground must be built on what the parent and teen truly share in common, not on what parents want to have in common. Biblical values are not a substitute for a life with Christ, but they represent the standard of conduct that conforms to God's moral laws.

Jesus Christ wants your child's heart. But it is hard to trust that God will win it. Somehow we think, *If I just share the right verse. If I just get him into the right youth group. If I just....*

Christian parents with teens who show a lack of surrender to Jesus Christ need to be careful with their words. By the teen years, their sons and daughters have already heard them many times. Let them instead see your words in action every day. Read

---

TRUE SALVATION

It's possible to raise a child who lives and acts morally but does not believe. However, it is impossible to raise a child who by his good works and moral living can gain entry into heaven (Isaiah 64:6; Romans 3:28). He or she needs to be saved.

The Bible says the place where God claims lost people is at the Cross. The Cross is where Jesus died the death that we by all rights should die and would die, apart from Him. Many teens raised in Christian communities have a clear knowledge of God but may not know Him personally.

Jesus Christ said, "I am the way, the truth, and the life. No one comes to the Father except through Me" (John 14:6). The Bible tells us that "He who has the Son has life; he who does not have the Son of God does not have life" (1 John 5:12). Furthermore, the Bible proclaims, "If you confess with your mouth the Lord Jesus and believe in your heart that God has raised Him from the dead, you will be saved. For with the heart one believes unto righteousness, and with the mouth confession is made unto salvation" (Romans 10:9–10).

your Bible. Parent your children, trusting God, not fearing circumstances. Pray and then pray some more.

Your goal, then, in parenting is to share the need for Jesus Christ, to instill godly moral values, and to build on this moral common ground. You aim for your child's heart but realize only God can reach it.

WHAT NOT TO DO

Dos and don'ts are both a part of moral training, but too often Christian families concentrate on the don'ts. Parents can get more occupied with suppressing wayward behavior in their teens than in elevating good. That is, when teaching moral precepts, we often tell our kids what is wrong and what not to do, rather than what is right and what to do. Compounding the problem is the preeminence we place on training during periods of conflict. Think about it for a moment—most parents tend to teach in moments of conflict when they tell their children what *not* to do, rather than in moments of peace when they can direct their children in what *to* do.

Negative moral training leaves a void that can cause serious moral compromise in the future. Because so much emphasis is placed on what to avoid and too little on what to do, the way to moral goodness is left undefined for the child. As a result, only the restraining half is internalized and not the half defining right living.

Certainly, suppressing the waywardness of a teenager's behavior is important, but when this is done without elevating good behavior, the parent ultimately ends up distorting what "good" really means.

For example, a child taught to be sensitive to other people's feelings has a stronger basis for future behavior than one merely taught to control his anger. Teaching our kids to do deeds of kindness is greater than teaching them not to be unkind. Restraining evil has to be balanced by elevating good. Moral restraint and moral assertiveness are two sides of the same coin. Both are needed in the training process.

Parents are in a position of great influence when it comes to helping their children internalize godly values. But how is that goal best achieved? Here are three considerations.

IT BEGINS WITH MOM AND DAD

When it came to developing a moral common ground, Moses had a whopper of a task. Hundreds of thousands of Israelites left Egypt with values turned and twisted by four hundred years of idols and false gods. In Deuteronomy 6:4–7, Moses told his people, "Hear, O Israel: The LORD our God, the LORD is one! You shall love the LORD your God with all your heart, with all your soul, and with all your might. And these words which I command you today shall be in your heart; you shall teach them diligently to your children, and shall talk of them when you sit in your house, when you walk by the way, when you lie down, and when you rise up."

Out of these four verses we can glean three principles of moral instruction. First, there is only one God to please, Jehovah God. He is an absolute God, and His commandments are consistent with His character. God is morally perfect, and all biblical values are an extension of His character. Potluck morality is out!

Second, the starting point of moral training begins with the parents. Moses said that before you diligently teach your children, "these words...shall be in your heart." If the principles of moral conduct do not reside in your own heart, you cannot pass them on to your children. It's a mistake to think moral training is the duty of the Sunday school, day school, or Christian school teacher. It is not! By intent or neglect, parents are the greatest moral influence on their children. Thus the words of Moses speak to the heart of the matter—the parents' heart.

Third, moral training is to take place during the normal activities of the day. "You...shall talk of them when you sit in your house, when you walk by the way, when you lie down, and when you rise up." By implication, moral truth is best communicated in periods of peace. That doesn't mean we will not teach at times of correction, but it does mean a healthy dose of moral enlightenment should take place throughout the day and in moments of peace when the child is not in a position to have to defend his or her actions.

The charge to parents from this passage is to know the God of moral truth, live His moral truth, and from that experience, teach your children that truth.

THE HOWS AND WHYS

It is not enough to teach your children how to *act* morally; you must also teach them how to *think* morally. To accomplish that goal, you need to think in accordance with biblical values. Moral thought is a prerequisite to the process of raising a morally responsible child.

A major reason children do not internalize values is because moral instruction too often lacks moral reason. By that we mean mothers and fathers often tell their children what to do, but they don't tell them why they should do it. That distinction must be emphasized because knowing how to do right and knowing why to do right are definitely two different things. The first speaks to moral action, the second to moral principle.

Many children know how to apply moral law, but not as many know the why behind it. When they go to church, children are told how to act; when they go to school, they are told to obey; when they go to grandma's house, they are told how to behave.

Thus, a greater emphasis is placed on the how-tos than the why-fors. As a result, some children reach adulthood appearing to be moral on the outside but lacking morality on the inside.

When we say parents should provide a "why" in their instructions, we don't mean parents are obliged to provide an explanation for every decision or instruction on demand. There will be times when the explanation "because Mommy said so" is enough. This is especially true in the toddler years. But after children have reached the age of three, parental instruction should become more characterized by the inclusion of the moral and practical reasons children should do what we tell them.

THE MORAL WHY

After morning services some of the kids from the junior high group began to ride their bikes on the church patio, in the midst of other churchgoers. When Ryan handed his Bible to his dad and headed toward his bike, his father stopped him and asked about Ryan's intentions. "I'm going to ride around the church with the guys," Ryan told him. His dad responded with "Ryan, I'm going to ask you not to do that." Then he did what is characteristic of proper biblical training: He gave his son the moral reason why.

Ryan's father explained that riding on the church patio was not appropriate because of the presence of others. He pointed out mothers with their babies, senior citizens coming and going (some with canes), folks in wheelchairs, and people chatting with hot coffee in their hands. He helped Ryan see the potential danger and explained why riding his bike in such circumstances was not morally acceptable. This time, dad governed Ryan's behavior; next time Ryan can do so on his own because the principle has been placed in his heart.

To further illustrate the importance of giving our kids the moral reason behind our instructions and restrictions, let's extend this hypothetical situation a bit further. Let's assume that Ryan's father denied him the opportunity to ride with his friends but never gave him the moral reason. We have found that when "no" is given without explanation, kids view the rule as applying only for today. Next week when Ryan's friends once again invite him to ride around the patio, Ryan will have no good reason *not* to ride—because no moral reason was placed in his heart.

If there is no principle to stir the heart, the heart will not be stirred. Children who do all the right things without knowing why they are right are moral robots. They often respond to situations and circumstances correctly, but not from any guiding principles of the heart. Getting the heart involved in life choices is an invaluable asset in adolescence. It is a prerequisite for you to lead your teens by your influence.

SHORT OF LEGALISM

In developing common moral ground, one thing to guard against is crossing into legalism. A legalistic approach to parenting is very dangerous, especially in the teen years. It leaves in its wake a frustrated teen. Legalism creates prohibitions by elevating the rule over the principle. The legalist sees all decisions in life as either black or white, immoral or moral. He or she acknowledges no heart or motive areas. No room is made for individual strengths and weaknesses. The legalist tends to demand that the consciences of all believers be identical.

We have all heard the exhortation "Let's keep things in context." The most notable aspect of a legalist is that he or she rejects context. Responding to the context of a situation does not mean we suspend biblical laws or principles; it means that we apply them in the most appropriate way. Considering context guards against legalism and helps a person determine how to confront the problem.

Context guards against legalism. Take Andrea's case. Her dad told her, "Honey, I don't want you to park the car on the street. Keep it in the driveway." He expected to be obeyed. But when the neighbor started to spray-paint his house and some paint drifted toward the car parked in the driveway, Andrea moved the car to the street.

The legalist would see that as a clear violation of the father's instruction, but Andrea's behavior did not violate the principle of caring for her dad's car. Context allows a child to do the right thing even if situations change. Failing to teach principle deprives the child of moral discretion.

The Bible represents ultimate authority and moral sufficiency. In its pages are the moral virtues that reflect God's righteousness and wisdom. There are no moral variations in its precepts. The values that govern conduct and define good and evil are the same for all people and for all time. As a parent, you need to realize that it is not enough to teach your teen how to act morally; you must also teach your child how to think morally. To accomplish that goal, you yourself must think in accordance with biblical values. That thinking is crucial to the process that you have begun—the process of raising a morally responsible child.

QUESTIONS FOR REVIEW

1. Think about what you've shared about Jesus Christ with each of your children. Describe the time you told each child about Christ's sacrificial death on the cross.

2. Think about your knowledge of the Bible. What can you do to maintain or increase your awareness of God's moral principles?

3. Write down three moral principles in your life. Where did they come from?

4. Do you agree that it is important to give moral and practical reasons for your directions? Why or why not?

5. Why is context so important in parenting?

CHAPTER SIX

Where Do I Begin?

When Dan and Laurie started attending our Reaching the Heart of Your Teen workshops, their daughter Melody wanted nothing to do with it. She told her mom and dad, "This is just one more way you're trying to get me to do what you want."

After the first few workshops, Dan and Laurie realized they'd been parenting in an authoritarian style. While talking with her husband, Laurie said, "I guess this is why Melody thought the workshops were just another way to control her. But what now? How do we change? And even if we do, how will Melody ever believe the change? Everything we try is going to be suspect."

Laurie wanted to know how to start over with credibility. This is a question that many parents ask. But before tackling the how, each parent must look at why he or she wants to start over.

Where is your relationship with your teen on the parent-teen continuum—joy-filled, conflict-filled, or somewhere in the middle? If your desire is to move closer to the positive end, consider whether you're truly asking, "Do I *wish* I could start over?" or "Am I *willing* to start over?"

Wish speaks to a fantasy of hope; willingness speaks to actual ability. As a Christian, you have the ability and the spiritual resources to start over with any relationship, and this certainly is true of the one between you and your child. Christ has made you complete (Colossians 2:10), He strengthens you and supplies your needs (Philippians 4:13, 19), and He has granted to you everything you need for life and godliness (2 Peter 1:3).

Christ has provided the tools for starting over, but are you willing and ready to use them? His expectations for us are high, and so should ours be. Your goal is not just to turn out OK kids who don't do drugs, who avoid trouble with the law, and who as adults manage to support themselves. Those accomplishments are important but are relationally meaningless. The possibilities are so much greater. Your goal is to create a hunger within your child to love and serve each family member. Your goal is to have a family that is characterized by the positive aspects of the first twenty questions of our survey in chapter 1. *The goal is relationship,* and it is never too late to start working on it. This is true whether your child is seven, seventeen, or twenty-seven.

Incidentally, the *you* and *your* in the previous sentences refer to parents as a team, as well as to individual parents. For optimal results, the two of you must engage in the cycle of change, willing to work toward a new relationship with your teen. But if you're a single parent or your spouse has an unwilling heart, don't lower your goal. Timothy became an outstanding and godly man because his grandmother and mother developed a close, moral-based relationship with him.

START WITH YOURSELF

Practically speaking, where should you begin? How do you go about mending relationship bridges which have been badly damaged? How do you change old habits of parenting this late in the game? How can you bring about positive moral changes, not just outward ones that placate you, but ones within your teen's heart?

The first step is often the most difficult of the entire journey.

Perhaps you made attempts in the past to reform your teen. Maybe you've tried discipline, grounding, rewards, the hard sell, the soft sell, the church youth group, sports, family counseling—and still there has been no improvement. Your efforts have resulted only in pain. You feel worried, helpless, hopeless, humiliated, and guilty. When the realization finally hits that you can't control your teen, despite all your efforts, you feel utterly defeated. Your relationship hurts, and you're discouraged. Can you, with God's help, really move from a negative to a positive relationship at this point?

We are convinced that when you make a sincere and sustained effort to change yourself first, other positive changes will occur. But it must start with you, the parent. You must be the initiator. Work to increase your influence. Become credible in the eyes of your teen. Do whatever is required to demonstrate your desire to change the status quo.

Learning how to manage your teen is secondary to learning how to lead your teen by your moral influence. That means you must take the lead in this quest and not give up. We'll deal with behavior management in later chapters, but for now, the goal is to build your credibility so you can lead by your influence, rather than by "laying down the law."

The rest of this chapter contains suggestions for helping you get started. Applying these suggestions now can help minimize further erosion, while creating a positive change in your relationship with your teen.

TELL GOD YOU WANT TO START OVER

Your heavenly Father knows everything there is to know about your family. He knows your pain, fears, and anxious moments. He delights when you, His child, ask Him for divine guidance. James, the brother of our Lord, reminds us of a simple truth: "You do not have because you do not ask" (James 4:2). Starting over with our children, regardless of their age, means approaching the Lord, inviting Him into our lives to reveal, expose, and change us.

In Psalm 139:23–24 David pleads with God, "Search me, O God, and know my heart; try me, and know my anxieties; and see if there is any wicked way in me, and lead me in the way everlasting." David wanted God to lay bare the sinful condition of his heart and to lead him up the path of righteousness.

Join David in this plea. Ask the Lord to reveal those things in your life that hurt Him. Then confess your sin—both unintentional and intentional. Either way, your sins and weaknesses must be brought to God. We all need a heavenly cleansing before we tackle our earthly problems. We must receive the Father's forgiveness and then His wisdom to parent effectively.

No parent purposely sets out to do an ineffective job of raising children. But many are misguided by the philosophies of this world and end up doing just that. There is forgiveness and hope. God understands your despair. Encourage yourself with these words: "If you say, 'Surely we did not know this,' does not He who weighs the hearts consider it? He who keeps your soul, does He not know it? And will He not render to each man according to his deeds?" (Proverbs 24:12). Tell God you're ready to start over.

FACE YOUR PAST

When God answers our prayers and exposes our sin, we must not stop there if our sin has touched other lives. The only way to get beyond our past is to seek forgiveness. Please note that asking for forgiveness doesn't mean saying, "I'm sorry." That phrase should be reserved for unintentional mistakes. For example, if you unintentionally step on your teen's model and break the wing off, you apologize, saying "I'm sorry." You may even pay to replace the model, but no malice was intended.

Seeking forgiveness, on the other hand, is different. We seek forgiveness when we knowingly do wrong—by deed, inactivity, or speech. To say "I'm sorry" is to acknowledge a mistake; to ask for forgiveness is to acknowledge wrong motives of the heart.

This distinction is very important. When we intentionally offend another, we have an obligation to seek forgiveness by asking for it, rather than declaring how sorry we feel. To simply say "I'm sorry" or "I apologize" is not enough. Sorrow is subjective and can range from little to great. Forgiveness is objective and has no middle ground—it's absolute. That means it is either sought or it's not. There is no such thing as partial or conditional forgiveness.

Our friend Allen seems to be in a perpetual state of war with his youngest daughter, Rebecca. The suggestion to start over by seeking forgiveness was not easy for him to accept. It wasn't a case of him rejecting the biblical injunction to forgive; he simply feared that admitting wrong would cause him to lose the little control he still had over Rebecca.

It is humbling and often extremely hard to seek out a teen who's hurt you and seek his or her forgiveness. But it is humility that begins to build credibility. It is humility that opens the door to leading by influence. It is humility that does not expect a preconceived response from your son or daughter. To admit to being wrong does not detract from a parent's authority or leadership. On the contrary, it teaches integrity. And it did work for Allen.

Seeking forgiveness for past mistakes should not be limited to you and your teen, but should extend to you and your spouse. It's easy to shift blame, to point a finger at someone and mumble, "We wouldn't have these problems if you listened to me and didn't give in as much." Or to say, "If you were around more, things would be different."

Each parent has contributed both positively and negatively to the present state of affairs. Each makes deposits toward healthy family advancements, and each contributes his or her share of mistakes. But blaming each other for the negative and staying silent about the positive is not going to help solve family problems. However, forgiving each other will (Matthew 6:14 and Luke 6:37–38).

Ask the Lord to give you the courage to confess to each other your weaknesses and your hidden patterns of fear. We encourage single parents to find a friend who can hold them accountable and encourage them along the way.

Confession and forgiveness can help break sinful patterns set in motion long ago. They afford an opportunity to start fresh. Do this for the sake of your relationships and for the sake of your children, remembering that your children will always be your children. Only death marks the ultimate deadline for reconciliation.

EXAMINE YOUR MARRIAGE

If you're together in a marriage, work on your husband-wife relationship, not just on your role as a mom or dad. Some people wonder, "What does our marriage have to do with our parent-teen relationship?" Answer? Everything.

Young children have an innate desire to know mom and dad love each other. That desire never leaves, not even when the child moves into adolescence and adulthood. If the husband-wife relationship is not visibly healthy, why should a teen emotionally invest in the family? If the two people leading the family can't get along, family renewal can hardly be expected.

Roger and Kim's thirteen-year-old son, Neil, demonstrated this truth. As a youth, Neil was out of control and troublesome. In desperation Roger and Kim sought help through a Growing Kids God's Way parenting class. But the challenge was to find someone to stay with Neil during their class. Because he could not be trusted to stay home alone and no one volunteered for the job, they brought their son to the church each week and sat him in the back of the auditorium while they sat in front, watching the video presentation.

In session three, the topic centered on the husband-wife relationship and the inherent need for children to know concretely that mom and dad love each other. That week's homework assignment directed parents to take fifteen minutes a day, when dad or mom comes home from work, and sit on the couch and talk as a couple. Such a simple task repeated daily, we explained, demonstrates to children in a tangible way mom and dad's friendship and togetherness.

After his parents had neglected their assignment for three weeks, Neil, in a moment of crisis, charged his parents with not loving him. "Why can't you give me what I really need? Why can't the two of you just sit on the couch and show me that you love each other? In three weeks you haven't done anything the man on the video said to do."

Apparently Neil was doing more than sitting in the back of the auditorium, reading his biker magazine. Out of his own desperation, he was listening to every word of the presentation, hoping for change.

It never occurred to Roger and Kim before that moment that even Neil understood this self-evident truth: Good marriages make for good parents. More than anything else they could do or say, their son wanted to know, "Do you love each other, Mom and Dad?" From that moment on, Neil was a changed teen, because his parents started to really love him by demonstrating their love for each other.

Every step taken to improve the marriage is a step toward strengthening the parent-child relationship, regardless of the age of the child. As you eliminate conflict in marriage, you eliminate conflict in parenting.

There is a definite correlation between strong marriages and successful parenting. The marriage relationship is the stage upon which the performance of trust is acted out before an audience of watchful eyes and hearts. The way your children see you loving and nurturing each other highly influences your believability.

There is a widespread myth that kids don't like to see their parents "act mushy." This is simply not true. Children—even teens—thrive on the demonstration of love between parents. They want the confidence that comes from knowing that dad and mom are tremendously in love with each other. A beautiful marriage makes family life attractive.

A father can be wonderfully active in the life of his children. He can take them hiking, fishing, skating, camping. He can help them with their homework and drive them to every possible school function. But he will undermine the security his good efforts should produce if he is not putting the same time and energy into loving his wife. Seeing dad neglect mom triggers the unconscious question, "What will keep Dad from neglecting me someday?"

In the same way, a mom can spend twenty-four hours a day with her children, being loving and sacrificial all the while. But her efforts have limited impact with her kids if she fails to demonstrate an unfailing love for her husband.

How much trust can a teen have in parents who won't take time to appreciate and be with each other? How much trust can a son or daughter have in a dad or mom who continually speaks harshly to his or her spouse, demonstrates a lack of patience, or manipulates the marital relationship? How can the child of parents in conflict be confident of their love for him or her while questioning their love for each other? Love between parents is basic to healthy family relationships.

ALLOW YOUR TEEN TO HELP
WITH YOUR WEAKNESSES

The idea of asking your teen to help you work on your weak areas may seem risky or frightening. But it has been proven to be an effective way of getting parent-teen relations on track.

Your teen has lived with you for thirteen to nineteen years, and believe me, he or she already knows your weaknesses. Being imperfect is easy for parents. Accepting that imperfection is harder. Inviting your teen to point out your weaknesses can be downright painful, yet it's necessary—both for your child and for you.

One characteristic of strong families is the freedom granted each member to lovingly confront one another when necessary. Sensitivity and wisdom must be applied if such interaction is to be effective. Both parties must be open to learning. And the individual being confronted must be willing to listen. The purpose of this confrontation is not to condemn but to strengthen; it is not to incite conflict but to provoke one another to love and good works (Hebrews 10:24).

The Holy Spirit provided the New Testament Church with a procedure permitting a believer to go to another in the Body of Christ to encourage and admonish him or her. This same strategy works for strengthening family relationships: "If a man is overtaken in any trespass, you who are spiritual restore such a one in a spirit of gentleness, considering yourself lest you also be tempted" (Galatians 6:1). Notice the guidelines. You are to employ a spirit of gentleness, and you are to remain aware of the power of sin over your own life.

We practiced this principle in our own family. As parents, we knew we had parenting blind spots—wrong perspectives, a lack of patience, occasional overconfidence in our decisions or too little confidence in our children's. We knew our teens saw all our frailties. They knew our strengths and weaknesses. Realizing that no one desired that we know the truth more than our own children did, we invited, even encouraged them to help us become better human beings. In doing so, we communicated to our children that we trusted them. We trusted their motives, and we trusted their discernment. That expression of trust spoke volumes to our daughters.

We didn't just let them "have at it," though. We set up some guidelines governing this privilege. Remember, although the following rules are written for teens confronting their parents, the same principles of respect can guide parents in confronting their teens.

1. Teens may not verbally assault their parents. They must speak honestly and honorably at all times.

2. Both teens and parents must be in agreement on the particular weakness or weaknesses to be worked on.

3. Teens must come with a desire to help, not to accuse.

4. Teens must be in control of their own attitudes when making an observation or accusation.

5. Struggling teens must want to start over. Their willingness to do so validates their desire to have a good relationship with mom and dad.

There are some advantages to giving your teens the freedom to work on your weaknesses. First, it fosters within you a healthy vulnerability. The popular notion is that vulnerability denotes weakness, but we're using the term to indicate strength. One of the keys to unlocking the door to the human heart is healthy vulnerability. To be vulnerable is to be open to the healthy censure or criticism of morally mature members of the family.

Vulnerability helps keep the inner person in check. It permits another person to hold up a mirror to us so we can see who we really are and who we are becoming. When we hold the mirror ourselves, we tend to look only at our good sides. Our teens are very good at showing us all sides. Teens detest hypocrisy in their parents; our vulnerability and openness to their input helps prevent it.

A second advantage develops when your teen makes an investment in the parent-teen relationship. What you invest in, you care about. This truth hit home when a relative persuaded us to invest in a European company doing business in the United States. We bought the company's stock at eighteen dollars a share. Within a month our stock had jumped to twenty-one dollars a share. Over the next several months, we watched our stock go up and down and back up again.

Getting involved in the stock market gave us a new appreciation for the word *investment*. Every day we found ourselves looking at the Dow Jones averages. Our attention turned from what we did initially with the investment, to what we wanted to do with it, to what we felt we must do. We guarded and nurtured our shares. We remained focused on the returns. The more growth we saw in our investment, the more committed we became. If our returns began to diminish, our investment received renewed attention.

The same is true of investments in relationships. Giving our teens the freedom to work on our weaknesses allows them an opportunity to invest relationally and emotionally in us as well. There is one clear truth about human nature and the nature of investment: People tend not to walk away from an investment that has cost a great deal. Personal investment gives us a reason to stick around—to nurture, watch, and add to our stock.

Your teen will do that with you. But first you must give him or her a healthy prospect of real rewards for the investment—

yourself. Are you willing to be vulnerable and open to investment? How is your relational portfolio? If you don't make yourself vulnerable, your teen has no pathway to your heart and no
hope of a healthy return.

DEVELOP YOUR ENCOURAGEMENT SKILLS

There is a big difference between uttering an occasional encouraging remark and being an encouraging parent. Real encouragement flows out of a relationship. It's more than a word now and
then; it's your very presence, smile, and expression that communicates encouragement.

It is easy to encourage a friend; it's much harder to encourage someone you're in conflict with. Yet encouragement means
more to a weakened relationship than to a strong one, especially
when it comes from a former foe. Continuous and honest
encouragement communicates a willingness to change the status
quo—a desire to move the relationship forward.

How about writing a little note? This is a practical way to
communicate encouragement. Think back to your childhood.
Did you ever receive a handwritten note from your dad or
mom—something beyond the usual Christmas and birthday-
card greetings, something simple, encouraging, and ending with
the precious words "I love you"? If so, you know how precious
such a gift can be. If you did not, it's likely that you can imagine
how such a gift could have made you feel.

It doesn't take much to occasionally tuck a note in with your
teen's lunch or schoolbook—maybe a thought or two on last
night's ballgame or the walk you took together. The time it takes
to write a twenty-word note is probably thirty seconds, but the
impact on your child can last a lifetime. The older the child, the
more he or she needs to hear encouraging words from you.

One step up from note writing is letter writing. Letter writing provides an excellent forum to communicate what really is on your heart. The very nature of expressing yourself with pen and ink allows you to select your words carefully, to qualify your thoughts, and to communicate your intent. Conveying your thoughts on paper is especially helpful when you know face-to-face communication often fails. Take time to express your concerns, struggles, and frustrations, plus the hopes, desires, and joys of your relationship.

No matter what style of communication you choose—words, notes, letters, or another form—take your teen's need for encouragement seriously. Don't wait for warning signs to tell you how much your teen needs you. On the surface, it may seem as though nothing in particular is claiming your child's attention. Or he or she may be dealing with issues that on the surface seem trivial. But to a teen in the midst of a trial, struggles that remain unspoken or are barely hinted at can be serious business. Many times parents underestimate a child's plea of urgency. Problems which appear trivial to us may seem insurmountable to them.

Listen for cues, and realize there will be some matters of major importance couched in insignificant-sounding statements. By listening carefully, you may be able to pick up on a serious problem your teen is having with a friend, teacher, or foe. Or you may get wind of a problem involving peer pressure. Seize these opportunities to encourage your teens through their difficulties by imparting your experience and wisdom. They need your help and encouragement, whether or not they will admit that to you.

STUDY YOUR TEEN

What makes your teen tick? What is his particular giftedness? What are his favorite pastimes? Does he like computers, sports, classical music, or the hum of a high-powered engine? If you haven't already, you must become a student of your teen. Learn to ask open-ended questions that require a thoughtful response. Rather than asking, "How is school going?" to which your child can reply, "Fine," try digging a little deeper. "What's the hardest part about your new math class?" "Are you and Sarah as close this year as you were in junior high?" "Who do you think is the cutest girl in school this year?"

You can gain tremendous insights by observing how teens live their lives. Teens, like adults, carry on an existence in three worlds: public, personal, and private. Their public world includes much of their time away from home such as that spent at school, work, and public events. Their personal world is much closer to home. Here teens live among family members, close friends, and relatives. It is within the secret chambers of the heart that we all live in our private world.

Your teen resides in all three worlds, and becoming a student of your teen means gaining access to all three. We found that growing to really know our own daughters required nothing less. Regular visits to each of their three worlds helped us maintain in our minds a composite sketch of who they were and who they were becoming.

We learned a great deal about our daughter Amy—about her sense of competition, fairness, and her attitudes about victory and defeat—by going to her junior and senior high school basketball games. How she lived her convictions on the court, in the locker room, and at practice added to our understanding of her complexity. Her public world provided a different window of observation from the ones through which we saw her most often. It gave us, as her father and mother, a more complete picture of who she is.

The same was true of our daughter Jennifer. She had a knack for handling money, finances, and investment. She knew more about the bond market at seventeen than either of us will ever know. Whenever we had a major family financial decision to make, Jennifer was always there, helping us work through the issues.

When you become a student of your teen, you have opportunities to borrow from their strengths. This, in turn, affirms them and strengthens your relationship with them.

In starting over with your teen, discover in which world your son or daughter spends most of his or her time. Does your son spend more time away from the family than in it? Is your daughter the type who keeps to herself, secretly finding security in her private world? The key to understanding your teen's public and personal worlds is to be in them when appropriate.

Sporting events, club activities, recitals, and school functions can give you access to your child's public world, but entry into his or her private world comes by invitation only. Quality time spent with the teen there can open the window to the private places of the child's heart. In our home, these special moments were planned as often as not. When we really wanted to hear from the kids or when they wanted to hear from us, we went out to lunch together to a neutral meeting place where we wouldn't be interrupted. Once there, we as parents listened with both our heads and our hearts.

Outside activities also provided opportunities for communication. Going for a walk with them, to a ballgame, out for a morning stroll through the mall, fishing, boating, or on a long bike ride together put us in close proximity, which is necessary for heart-to-heart sharing. Don't rely upon chance meetings to hear from your children. Plan for those times, and make those opportunities happen.

GUARD YOUR TONGUE AND TONE

There is an old axiom that says, "Think before you speak." Another way to say this is: Learn to measure your thoughts against your teen's excitement. Gary had to learn this the hard way. You see, he's the type of person who does not like radical change, especially if there is no warning. So you can imagine the scene in our home some years ago when our teenage daughters waltzed into the room, bouncing new permed curls. "Dad, how do you like our hair?"

Gary stared, allowing his senses to take it all in. Then he said something dumb like "Does your mother know you did that?" Once uttered, those words could not be called back. Nor could he return to two pretty faces the hope that Dad, the most important man in their lives, would share in their fun and excitement of the moment. His tongue and tone robbed their hearts.

As parents, we sometimes make rash decisions without thinking of the potential consequences of our choices. If you want to rebuild your relationship with your teens or just manage them with emotional gentleness, guard your tongue and your tone. Measure your responses against the excitement on your teens' faces. Do this before they decide you are not to be trusted with the joys of their lives.

BUILD FAMILY SUPPORT

Each member of a family must learn to communicate honestly and listen attentively. Are you willing to provide opportunities for your children to talk as you listen to them? Here are five practical suggestions to help cultivate that all-important alliance.

Share at least one meal together as a family each day.

To live with a teen is to live in the fast lane. With all that is going on in their lives—school, sports, youth group, club activities, socials, friends, and employment—scheduling family time when everyone can be there is a challenge.

We know how difficult that can be. When our children

reached their teen years, life became a conflict of schedules. After-school activities put pressure on what had once been a very predictable family life. It seemed that whenever we were pulling into the driveway, one of the kids was pulling out, on her way to her next event.

Because time demands can loosen family ties and seriously strain already weak ones, extra effort must be put into keeping the family together. That's why we committed ourselves to regrouping each night at mealtime. Sometimes that meant our schedules had to change, and sometimes theirs did. But we were committed to having one meal together each day—to relax, talk, recharge our emotional batteries, find out what was going on in one another's lives, and enjoy our growing friendship with our teenagers.

Read after dinner.

Reading together is becoming a lost family art, yet it is one of the most pleasant activities that can be shared between parents and children of all ages. After dinner each night, before the dishes were cleared from the table, Anne Marie led our family in a story time. It was one of our best pastimes. George Mueller, D. S. Moody, Hudson Taylor...one chapter a night allowed us to walk with the great men and women of the Christian faith.

Reading together after dinner did more than add to our minds. It was during times like these that we really gave our children what they needed—a sense of family identity built upon the memories of our togetherness. If you're starting over, reading after a meal is one good place to begin.

Allow your teens to plan a family night.

Some people think having leisure-time activities with your children is a luxury. It is not a luxury; it's an absolute necessity. Family night helps keep your work and play in perspective. We planned a family night once a week. It was a time when we separated ourselves from work and school and came together for family fun. Family night afforded us an informal setting for relaxing with family members who didn't care how our hair looked or what we were wearing.

We eventually added a little twist to our weekly family fun night. Long before our children reached their teen years, they took ownership of every other family night. They prepared a budget and planned the evening. We played board and card games, had indoor picnics or feasted on pizza and fondue, and watched a favorite video classic.

What are the benefits? Your children are not just taking ownership of a family night every other week; they are actually taking ownership of your family. It is their investment in the fun portion of other family members' lives. It adds another good reason for them to stick around. Plan family nights. This ensures that your children don't end up with your leftover time.

Let them participate in building family memories.

Not only can you encourage your teen to plan a family night, you can take the next step and encourage him or her to help you plan the next family vacation. Whether it is a short weekend camping trip with your church Sunday school or a week-long event away from home, planning and participating adds a positive memory-building dimension for your teen. The more healthy the memories, the closer you grow as an interdependent family.

Building memories with your children means more than taking them places and doing fun things with them. It requires that they become participants in all aspects of the activity. Some friends of ours realized this truth many years ago. For years they had left the February cold of northern New England to spend two weeks in warm Florida. Each year our friends returned home discouraged by their children's constant complaints and lack of appreciation for all that the parents felt they had done.

Then one year someone suggested they let their kids help plan the next family trip. That included letting them help decide the travel route, make some of the scheduling decisions, and select some of the special events they would attend along the way. It made all the difference in the world.

What made the difference? The children became participants in the vacation instead of spectators. And the overall benefit? The work that went into planning and scheduling, the anticipation of seeing those plans realized, and the sense of ownership all built lasting memories for each member of that family.

Take walks together.

If your response to this is, "Yeah, right—three hundred years ago," give it a chance. It may surprise you that this simple suggestion may be accepted. We found that taking walks with our daughters—one at a time—brought about conversations we otherwise would not have had. There is something about a twenty-minute walk that causes people to reflect, open up, and share their hearts. Those moments of reflection often led to very personal and private conversations with our girls.

Walking with our children gave them access to us and gave us access to them. They exposed their inner thoughts, fears, doubts, and hopes. Sometimes they just needed to talk, which meant those walks were good times for us to just listen. Not everything we heard made sense to us, but that was all right. We knew our listening served a purpose; it provided a sounding board to help our children sort things out. On occasions like that, we would often hear a heartfelt "Thanks for listening, Mom and Dad." Those meaning-rich words warmed our hearts every time we heard them.

Dining, reading, planning, playing, walking together.... This is just a partial list of the activities we have enjoyed together as a family. Make your own list. See if you can come up with ten options. What are your individual family members' favorite activities? Choose one or two to do together this week. Then do them!

LIVE YOUR CHRISTIANITY

One last credibility builder is your own personal integrity. Healthy families govern themselves from a clear set of values. For the Christian, these values are biblical. At least they are supposed to be.

Probably one of the most destructive forces in parenting a teen is hypocrisy. Parental hypocrisy occurs when mom and dad exempt themselves from the set of values they require their children to uphold. This double standard happens when you tell your kids church is important but then you tear down the service or other members while driving home. It happens when you tell your kids never to steal but you don't return a clerk's accidental overpayment of change. Hypocrisy breeds contempt, leading to relationship breakdown.

For our family, the Bible was the final authority. The Word of God was the umpire that settled all our disputes. Only biblical ethics provide the safeguards needed to prevent parents from becoming hypocrites because only a biblical approach calls both parent and child to accountability. That is, the moral rules that apply to our children also apply to us.

Solomon said it is the little foxes that destroy the vineyard (Song of Solomon 2:15). The little acts of hypocrisy that may have gone undetected in your child's early years stand out as beacons during the teen years. Parental hypocrisy dismembers the family. If you're starting over or just desiring to improve your parent-teen relationship, don't just preach your Christianity; live it.

BEGIN TODAY

Are you willing to start over? If so, there are a few things you should consider as you begin the process of re-parenting and relationship-building. First, gather everyone together for a family conference. Reveal the mistakes you've made in the past, then seek your children's forgiveness. Next, discuss what God requires of parents and children. Don't skip over his expectations of you! If the issue is obedience, what does God require in that area? If it is respect, what does His Word say about that? Share how your family has not been functioning according to biblical ethics, and establish a common ground from which all family members will work in the future. Explain the new course of action that all of you will be undertaking.

Finally, after answering all their questions, join together in prayer, asking the Lord to give you and your teen the wisdom to do what is right with a fresh new beginning.

The key to starting over is consistency. When you start over as a family, your teens will scrutinize you and your spouse from a distance to see if there are any changes. Do everything you can to make your efforts count. By God's grace, you can and will achieve a new beginning with your teen.

QUESTIONS FOR REVIEW

1. Are you a good encourager? Is your marriage strong? Review this chapter's credibility builders. What do you believe is your strongest point? your weakest? What can you do to improve?

2. What is easier for you to say: "I'm sorry" or "Will you please forgive me?" Why? What would you like to do differently after reading this chapter?

3. Review our ideas for building family support. Now go over your own list of activities you and your family can participate in together. Decide which one you will try this week, and set a date.

4. Biblical ethics provide safeguards that help prevent parental hypocrisy. Write down the ones you are studying and learning from the Bible.

CHAPTER SEVEN

Making Relationship a Family Affair

Not long ago, we planned a vacation that included both of our married daughters and their families. For a week, we enjoyed Lake Meade on a rented houseboat. Within the confines of our on-the-water home, we swam, fished, read, relaxed, and in general had an incredibly good time. So good, in fact, that while traveling home Amy suggested, "We ought to do this again."

Everyone chimed in with, "Oh, yeah! Let's do it." "I get two weeks off next year." Before we reached our different homes, most of the plans were made to repeat our houseboat vacation.

The friendship of our adult children is a parenting dividend we didn't give much thought to while changing diapers or reading Bible stories. But as children turn into teens, it's important to ask these questions: When my children become old enough to select their own friends, will they have any reason to choose mom and dad or their sisters and brothers? Do my children consider their family part of their inner circle of most loyal friends?

Other questions also give insight into the relationship bonds being created within your home. What will our family identity be in another three, five, or ten years? Have we cultivated a team spirit in our home? Have we instilled a God-honoring value system in our children's lives? Who else is raising our children?

Family structures promote or hinder healthy parent-teen relationships as well as relationships between siblings.

TOGETHER OR ALONE?

Even in the closest and most natural of human relationships, that between a parent and child, there is no guarantee of future rapport. Though both parties contribute to the strong or poor outcomes in the relationship, for the most part, parents remain in the driver's seat. They can control or greatly influence the outcome by the choices they make. One such choice deals with family structure. Are you an interdependent or an independent family? The first is more desirable; the second is dangerous. Let's look at each in turn.

INTERDEPENDENT VS. INDEPENDENT

Please take note of the prefix *inter-* in the word *interdependent.* Like threads in a tapestry or two-by-fours in the frame of a house, each individual part supports the others in order to create a whole. The relationship of each thread or board to the others is mutual. In the same way, each member of the *interdependent* family is mutually dependent upon each other.

This can be further illustrated by a group of people holding hands while in a circle and facing inward. This arrangement is the best possible one for sending and receiving family values. These values are communicated and demonstrated by mom and dad. They're sent to the children, shared with each other, and sent back again to mom and dad. Due to steady parental influence, the standards of moral conduct for each family member are established primarily within the home.

Interdependency should not be confused with the popular counseling term *codependency.* When problems arise in interdependent relationships, the issue is confronted, and each individual seeks to restore the whole. When problems arise in codependent relationships, fear and insecurity produce behavior that covers up the issue and functions around it.

Interdependent relationships provide satisfaction, protection, and security in the early years, and they serve as a barrier against intrusive values in the teen years. The interdependent family cultivates a sense of belonging, which leads to allegiance to one another and allegiance to the core values of the family. Children grow with a "we-ism" attitude regarding their families rather than the selfish "me-ism" attitude that leads to lonely independence.

In contrast, an *independent* family structure is one in which each family member is free from the influence, guidance, and control of another. Family members are unaffiliated, alienated, and uncommitted to one another—in short, they stand alone.

Again, we can use a circle analogy to describe this structure. Like the interdependent family, the independent family also is holding hands while standing in a circle. But that is where the similarity ends. Instead of all members looking in toward one another, each member looks out, away from the center.

The independent family looks unified from a distance, but it is far from what a family should be. Everyone is caught up in his or her own little world, doing his or her own independent thing. As a result, children turn to their peers more by default than by choice.

On paper, most people would choose the interdependent family structure. Everyone wants to belong, to be supportive, and to be supported. But for the structure to work in real life, it means sacrifice. It means being there for one another. As parental heads of the home, it means the process begins with us.

There will always be better jobs, higher positions, deeper classes, more convenient gyms, and greater opportunities for self-growth and enrichment. These are all good, and it is hard to say no to them. But when parents no longer have time to fulfill their role as their children's primary moral influence, the resulting vacuum will be filled with the voices of public institutions and their children's peers. The inevitable result for the children is increased alienation, indifference, and independence.

You cannot expect family harmony when other people are socializing your kids with their values. The stronger the outside influences in the early years, the greater the potential division in the teen years.

CONSEQUENCES OF DESIGN

Examining these two family structures in action leads to some interesting conclusions. Children who receive comfort and approval from the intimate and dependable relationships found in the interdependent family tend to look to those same or similar relationships as they move through adolescence.

In contrast, a child who is weaned by outside influences and dependent on peers for the satisfaction of basic social needs is more likely to grow up being sensitive to group pressures and disapproval. The tendency is to move in the direction of peers and become indifferent to non-peer influences such as parents. This is the way of the independent family.

Unfortunately, we have been led to believe that teens naturally seek an identity independent of their parents, regardless of family structure. We hear of sons and daughters who turn away from their families, looking more to peers than to their parents to establish their own identity. In order to deal with this belief, we need to understand what exactly adolescent identity is.

WHO AM I?

Identity association is not a psychological invention developed in the halls of academia. It is a life-on-life dynamic found in all human relationships. It is a socializing process by which a person identifies with a group he or she is familiar with, attracted to, or feels empathy with. We derive from our identity associations our sense of belonging, and we give back to these affiliations varying degrees of allegiance.

Everyone has a potpourri of identity associations that provide a sense of belonging and allegiance. Some of these connections are casual and loosely tied, while others are intimately linked with us. For example, every four years we identify with our Olympic athletes. By proxy, they compete for us. When they win, we win; when they lose, we lose. We also can identify with pain, hurt, and grief. Mothers and fathers who have lost a child to a drunk driver identify emotionally with members of MADD (Mothers Against Drunk Driving). If a parent has lost a baby to SIDS (Sudden Infant Death Syndrome), there is an identity link with the members of the SIDS Foundation. Closer to home, we identify with clubs, ethnic groups, professions and trades, local sports teams, churches and denominations, circles of friends, and of course, our own families.

Each of us has a number of identity associations to which we pledge a degree of allegiance and devotion and from which we receive an affirmation of belonging. So it is with teenagers and their identity associations.

IDENTITY IN CHRIST

To be a Christian is to be identified with Jesus Christ. Jesus says in John 13:35, "By this all will know that you are My disciples, if you have love for one another." With that statement, Jesus establishes love as the identifying characteristic that sets His people apart from the world. The apostle Paul said believers are identified with Christ in His death, resurrection, ascension, and reign. A synonym for *identity* is the word *union*: "You in Me, and I in you" (John 14:20).

Viewed in this manner, identity is fundamental to unity.

Being part of a group identity does not take away from our individual uniqueness. In 1 Corinthians 12:20, the apostle Paul makes this point by saying, "But now indeed there are many members, yet one body." A person's identity with a group does not take away from that person's individuality. Actually, each choice to identify with something or someone is an extension of individuality. So it is in the Christian family. We are all individuals tied to a corporate identity in Christ.

THE DEFINING CONNECTION

Identity defines us by providing a set of socially understood reference points. A parish priest, for example, has a religious identity revealed in his clothing, speech, and lifestyle. The rock musician also is recognized by his clothing, speech, and lifestyle. They both have an identity that complements their values, and they both are identified by what they believe and how they act. People don't look at the rock musician and say, "Ah, there goes a religious man." Nor do they look at the priest and say, "There goes a pop-rock vocalist."

What or whom we associate with reveals who we are and what we believe. But there is more to it than just an outward association. Identity also promotes a sense of belonging. We feel more comfortable among like-minded people who uphold, justify, and support the existence of our values. In contrast, we feel isolated and sometimes threatened by groups that do not share our values. For this reason, we all tend to seek relationships with others who agree with our values. This is definitely true of teens.

THE BOND OF SHARED VALUES

Values either unify or divide people. Common values foster harmony and peace; opposing values can produce civil war. The more similar our values, the closer we tend to draw to people. The more values differ, the more people separate from each other. This holds true for families, parents, and teens; and it is the reason values-based parenting is highly successful. Parenting from a foundation of common values builds on the natural tendency of children to associate with their parents, gain a sense of belonging, and pledge their allegiance to the family.

In strong families, adolescence is not a time when teens seek new identities. Rather, they attempt to validate the ones they already have. Unless driven away by the influences described in this and earlier chapters, teens don't seek primary identities apart from their families.

There is no hidden, genetically controlled, instinctive dynamic that causes teens to automatically reject their parents and family in favor of peers. This is good news for family relationships.

PEERS AND THE INTERDEPENDENT FAMILY

Among behavioral scientists, it is commonly accepted that teens are driven by a natural quest to find their own identities and that they use peers to help establish and then validate what they believe. However, that's not true of teens who are members of an interdependent family.

Within the comfortable confines of the interdependent family, parents—not peers—usually have the greater influence. The very nature of progressive development reveals that teens choose their community identities—that is, their peer friends—only after their family identities are first established and then accepted or rejected. If the family is accepted as the primary source of values and comfort, then the teen not only identifies with but makes friends from among those possessing similar values. This creates positive peer pressure. When there is harmony between the core beliefs of parents and teens, then both seek similar values in other families and friends. That is why, ultimately, peer pressure on a child is only as strong as family identity is weak.

The closer the values between parents and teen, the stronger the allegiance and the less likely that the teen will drift away from the parents. Once again, we need to realign thinking that has been skewed by popular belief: It isn't the power of peer pressure that tears adolescents from their parents; rather, it is a conflict in values that makes teens more vulnerable to peer pressure.

Please note that the strong family does not eliminate normal peer pressure as much as it develops healthy ways to deal with it. This is why it is wrong to blame peer pressure as the primary cause of drug use, crime, rebellion, sexual promiscuity, and the general breakdown of the family. Fundamentally, the problem is a matter of incompatible values.

PEERS AND THE INDEPENDENT FAMILY

There is a natural inclination for young children to identify with their families. There is good reason for this. For most children, the home environment is their greatest source of satisfaction, protection, and security. It isn't until they enter adolescence that peer pressure takes on maximum significance for kids. It is also during this period that prior parenting strengths and weaknesses are revealed.

Unlike the interdependent family, an independent family structure tends to promote incompatible values. When parents limit the fullness of their relationship with their children during their children's formative years—birth through age twelve—by encouraging development of the independent family structure, the child upon reaching adolescence is more prone to seek an identity apart from his parents. He needs to fit somewhere. When the family is rejected and Christ is rejected, the teen is left with only his peer group to validate his beliefs.

To ensure peer acceptance, the teen learns that he must accept the group's interests and values. He cannot afford to be different because this would jeopardize his status within the group. To demonstrate his allegiance, he acts out his new association and conforms to the group's identity. This might be represented by choices in hairstyle, clothes, music, and the use of slang or foul language. Rejecting parents also becomes part of the teen's expression of group identity. Recovery, then, is made more difficult by the fact that teens react more readily to the approval and disapproval of their peers than to the approval and disapproval of their parents.

THE PASSIVE REBELLION WEDGE

More subtle than negative peer pressure but just as destructive to parent-child relationships is passive rebellion. Passive rebellion in teens is much like passive rebellion in young children. A child may be sitting down on the outside but not necessarily sitting down on the inside. Similarly, a teen can privately reject the family but publicly stay in touch with it—at arm's length. Passively rebellious teens are antagonistic to their parents' beliefs, but for any number of possible reasons, they are not ready to confront their parents with their own values.

Many teens wait until they are "out of the house" to reveal their true views because they don't feel safe expressing them while living at home. This is a dangerous situation. Like a virus, the sickness may spread, consume the host, or amount to nothing at all. These teens conform for conformity's sake until one day they simply are gone.

Passively rebellious teenagers reject their parents by moving into sports, clubs, or other group activities that provide a safe distance from their parents. They may even find their primary identity in a church youth group rather than their own family.

Belonging to a youth group for some teens is a way of placating the parents by tolerating their values. Unfortunately, the problem becomes even more complex when youth ministries resemble *parafamilies*. A youth worker should not become the spiritual authority in a teen's life instead of parents. This betrays the family and undermines its leadership.

The message "Your parents don't understand what you're going through, but we do" is divisive and does nothing to encourage family unity. Such statements actually justify teen antagonism by adding an air of legitimacy to any relational conflict. From a teen's perspective, "You don't understand me" serves both to justify and motivate further deterioration of ties to the parents' values.

EVALUATING A YOUTH MINISTRY

To help determine if your teen's youth group aids or detracts from your family's health, consider the following four questions:

1. Does the youth staff support parental authority by encouraging and verbally praising time spent with the family?

2. Does the youth staff support parental authority by notifying you when teaching on sensitive sexual matters?

3. Does the youth staff support leadership by not overriding mom and dad's authority?

4. Does the youth staff promote the parent-teen relationship by speaking well of parents and helping them understand teen problems?

If you answered "no" to any of these questions, consider approaching the youth staff. Often the problem is simply youthful, but misdirected zeal on the part of a worker and not a cognitive desire on his or her part to undermine parental influence and leadership in the home. Their motives may be right, but their methods wrong. However, if the problem goes deeper, consider another youth program.

QUESTIONS FOR REVIEW

1. Take a few minutes to think about your family structure. Is it independent or interdependent? List some strengths and weaknesses of your structure.

2. Does your family have a Christian identity? Explain your answer.

3. List some of the associations in your life that give you identity. List some of your teen's.

4. Write down two things that give your family a sense of belonging.

5. Think about why you agree or disagree with the following statement:

"It is not the power of peer pressure that tears adolescents from their parents but a conflict in values that makes teens more vulnerable to peer pressure."

PART III

OPENING THE

lines of

COMMUNICATION

CHAPTER EIGHT

Learning to Say, "I Love You"

In our family we joke about "ums." "UMS" is a little-known condi-tion usually found in individuals on days when everything goes wrong—from getting cut off on the freeway to getting called in for a "little talk" with the boss. UMS stands for "Ugly Mood Syndrome," and on this particular day, Gary had a bad case of it. Anne Marie and Jennifer weren't around when he got home, but eighteen-year-old Amy was out in the garage working on a project. When her father found her, she grinned and said, "Hi, Dad. You're home."

Normally, Gary would respond to this innocent greeting in kind, but on this day, the pressures of his afternoon got the best of him, and he unfortunately showed it. "Amy, what are these boxes doing in the garage? How many times have I told you girls I want them kept on the shelves? And there is Styrofoam everywhere. I want this mess cleaned up right now! Is that my good hammer?"

What happened next is still hard to believe. It took a lot of courage and even more love. Amy put down her project and walked over to Gary. Then she put her arms around him, held him for a moment, then wispered, "You must have had a hard day, Dad. You need a hug."

LOVE BEYOND THREE WORDS

It wasn't easy for Amy to love her father that day, because in that moment he was anything but loveable. Some days it isn't easy for parents to love their teens. But love is not an option for Christians. It is a command. In John 13:34 Jesus says, "A new commandment I give to you, that you love one another; as I have loved you, that you also love one another."

Jesus Christ is an example of purest love—the best example there has ever been. He left heaven's splendor to come to earth and die for mankind (Philippians 2:6–8). As He loved, we are to love. It's as simple and as complex as that. Knowing how to love as Jesus loves is vital to showing our teens and others the truth of Christ. In John 13:35 Jesus says, "By this all will know that you are My disciples, if you have love for one another." Love is the badge that identifies us as disciples of Jesus Christ. God wants us to love one another so the world will know we belong to Him. And the place to learn about love is in the Christian home.

TWO-SIDED LOVE

Love has two sides: giving and receiving. Giving love is the action side; receiving love is the feeling side. For some people, love is an action void of feeling; they just do "love." For others, it is a feeling void of action; there is talk of "love," but no demonstration of it. Not having a balance in love is what ultimately makes the process of loving frustrating.

Actions and feelings, in the context of love, do not need to conflict with each other. Jesus was not emotionless. He loved in action and with feeling. His love in action led Him to die for us. His feelings of love were demonstrated with tears at the death of His friend Lazarus (John 11:35). Actions and feelings are part of the equation of love, and like other biblical truths, both are often violated.

We all recognize that one of the deepest emotional desires we have is to feel loved. God made us to be both rational and emotional creatures. He gave us the capacity to feel loved and, equally important, the ability to choose to demonstrate it. But it can be frustrating because we're not always sure our actions are interpreted as love. The question we must somehow find the answer to is this: How can I demonstrate love in action so that the person I am directing it toward actually senses love?[7]

We know that parents naturally love their children. We also know they can become frustrated in that love. They try many different ways of saying "I love you," but sometimes there is no evidence that the child feels or appreciates that love. It may seem that the harder parents try, the less the child values the effort.

Many parents have a wrong view of how to express love to their teens. They sometimes believe that giving their teens anything they want, when they want it, is a way of saying "I love you." Appropriate gift-giving can be a valid expression of affection for a child, but extravagant giving on demand does not demonstrate love—certainly not biblical love. Such expressions will never lead teenagers to feel good about themselves or loved by their parents.

We need to learn how to say "I love you" in ways that get our message into the hearts of our children, filling their emotional needs. Authentic expressions of love will cause your teen to say the same right back to you.

LOVE LANGUAGES

Love is expressed through emotional languages. A love language is the ability to express love and concern to another person in the primary emotional language of that person. Gary better understood this need to express love in the other person's primary love language when he was in the former Soviet Union and had the opportunity to visit Red Square.

As he was walking through the square, he noticed that a crowd had assembled to watch the changing of the guard at

Lenin's tomb. The people who were gathered there spoke Russian, their native tongue. Since it wasn't Gary's native language and he didn't know how to speak it, the words held no meaning to him. The sound receded to a hum in his ears. As the replacement guards started their march toward the tomb, he suddenly heard off to his left, "Hey, Larry! Come over here. You can get a great picture!" Instantly his head turned.

Gary tuned in right away because someone was speaking his native tongue, English. Even if someone had spoken in Spanish, he would have paid attention. It isn't his native language, but having lived in southern California, where that language is often spoken, he would have identified it. Not as quickly as English, but he would have identified it since Spanish is his second-strongest language. French is his third. He doesn't register its meaning as quickly and misses some words, but he has some understanding of it. The point is this: The languages we are most familiar with are the ones we readily tune in.

What happens with spoken languages also happens with emotional languages. We may speak our primary emotional language, but it often comes across to other people as an unknown tongue. We say "I love you" in one language, while they say it in another. As a result, our efforts to demonstrate love are frustrated. When this happens within our families, we are tempted emotionally to walk away from our children and our mates, thinking no one cares about our attempts to love. To avoid this frustration, we need to learn the five basic languages of love and discover which one is the "native tongue" of each family member.

Love Language One: Encouraging Words

The apostle Paul identified the power of love when he told the Corinthians that love edifies or "builds up" (1 Corinthians 8:1). One way of expressing love is by building up others through verbal encouragement. "You're such a compassionate person; I could learn a lot from you." "The flower garden looks beautiful. You must have worked on it all day." "That dress really looks terrific on you." But these words will only touch the heart if they are sincere. Flattery is not encouragement.

Taking the time to verbally pat someone on the back is a way of saying, "I love you." For some, there is no greater way to express love than with words of legitimate praise and recognition.

Love Language Two: Acts of Service

The apostle John encouraged Christians to love with action and in truth (1 John 3:18). That is another way of communicating love, through sincere acts of service. This means doing something special for another person, something you know he or she will appreciate. Normally, this is something outside the realm of everyday routine. For a husband, this may be putting gas in his wife's car on Sunday night so she doesn't have to worry about filling the tank that week. Or maybe he will express his love by fixing the leaky faucet or by making the shelves his wife wants in the closet.

When a husband comes home from work, believing the patio needs sweeping and finding it already done by his wife, he has a heightened appreciation of his wife on the basis of that act of love—especially if his primary love language is spoken in acts of service. Because he didn't expect it, the act means more to him. He is aware that she did it because she knew how much he would appreciate it. Whenever you do something for another person beyond the normal course of events, you are saying "I love you" in action.

Love Language Three: Gift-giving

The greatest gift of love the world has ever known is Jesus Christ, who gave Himself for His Church (Ephesians 5:25). Gift-giving is a third way of saying, "I love you." Even simple or no-cost gestures can convey great meaning because of what they represent.

Impromptu gift-giving (unlike giving gifts on occasions such as birthdays or holidays, when they are expected) sends the message "When we are apart, you are on my mind. This gift is a token reflecting my thoughts of you." The message goes even deeper into the heart when the gift is the other person's favorite color or something he or she collects. This type of gift carries the message "I'm paying attention to you and noting what you care about."

A modest gift is a meaningful token that can say to a discouraged heart, "I love you."

Love Language Four: Quality Time

The gospel record provides insights into the quality time Jesus had with His heavenly Father and with the men He discipled. Although His goal was to train His disciples for ministry service, He recognized that they needed to spend personal time with Him.

We can begin to define quality time by stating what it is not. It is not sitting on the couch, reading the newspaper or watching television together. Quality time requires that you invest yourself in the other person—your child or spouse. It includes listening carefully and responding appropriately. It involves two people who are actively participating in a conversation and going beyond simply communicating facts. The time spent at this may be only ten minutes, but for the person whose love language is quality time, those ten minutes are precious.

Love Language Five: Physical Touch and Closeness

Think of what it must have been like to be one of the children described in Mark 10:13–16. Jesus gathered them in His arms and blessed them, using the children and their love as an object lesson for His disciples.

> **FOUR TRUTHS ABOUT LOVE LANGUAGES**
>
> 1. Your primary love language is evident in two ways: You speak it more often than the other languages, and you feel most loved when it is spoken to you.
>
> 2. You have the ability to speak all five languages, and you need to speak them all.
>
> 3. By age seven, a child's primary love language has developed sufficiently to be recognizable. Love languages may begin to emerge before seven years, but they're more difficult to distinguish and to assign a priority ranking. Of course, all children under seven like presents, hugs, and quality time.
>
> 4. The most important point to remember is this: Every day we choose to love or not to love. Choosing to love your mate in his or her love language is a greater act of love than exercising your own primary language. Jesus loves us when we are least lovely, and we should be willing to do the same, loving one another "Even as I have loved you" (John 13:34b).

Within the context of a marriage relationship, some spouses assume that because they enjoy lovemaking, their primary love language must be physical touch. This is not the case. The language of physical touch and closeness is more far-reaching than that. It is a special way of saying, "I love you." Holding hands, putting your arm around your spouse's or child's shoulder, warm hugs, or just standing close to each other can telegraph a special love message.

Here is another example of this love language: A husband is working in the garden, and his wife sits down nearby with a book and begins to read. She could have read the book anywhere in the house, but she chose to be close to her husband. This, too, transmits a message of love. Some couples enjoy being near each other even when silence prevails. Simply knowing the other person is nearby can confirm a partner's affection and care.

WHAT LANGUAGE DO YOU SPEAK?

Of the five love languages, one is your primary language. One of these modes of expression means more to you than the other four, and another means the least to you. Your primary love language is the one you most enjoy having expressed to you and the one you tend to "speak" to others. However, learning how best to say "I love you" in the primary language of your spouse or child often means stretching beyond what you prefer to what the other prefers.

Scenario One

Bill and Sally had a good Christian marriage, yet the full sensation of love was missing. They knew they loved each other but also felt frustrated in communicating it. It turned out that Bill's primary love language was physical touch and closeness. He spoke that language and felt loved when it was spoken to him. The language that meant the least to him was words of encouragement. In contrast, encouraging words was Sally's primary language, and the last on her list was physical touch and closeness.

This couple loved each other but didn't know how to communicate their love in a common language. Bill often asked his wife, "How about a hug?" In turn, Sally wished that Bill would write her more notes and letters as he had when they were dating. She wanted to hear words of encouragement, while he desired physical touch and closeness. For example, if Sally worked hard in the front yard, she hoped that when Bill walked through the door he would say, "The rose garden looks beautiful. Thank you for your efforts." Bill did walk by the garden and appreciate her work, but he rarely communicated his pleasure in her primary language, words of encouragement.

At a seminar addressing the five love languages, Bill and Sally learned that every day each of us chooses whether or not to communicate love. When they understood that basic truth, each of them chose to love the other in his or her primary language. Bill now says "I love you" with words of encouragement. He leaves notes around the house or calls his wife during the day. He now chooses to communicate love verbally. Sally, too, has chosen new ways to express her love. She now speaks his language of physical touch and closeness. She initiates hand holding and hugs, and she stands close to Bill during social gatherings. Because they both have chosen to love in accordance with the other's primary language, the fullness of love has returned to their marriage.

Scenario Two

Dave's primary love language is acts of service; Ruth's is quality time. Here is a typical example of how this difference affects their time together. After work, Dave comes through the door, embraces his wife, and receives an invitation to sit and talk before dinner. Dave agrees and suggests that Ruth make some coffee while he changes his clothes. Ruth goes to the kitchen to prepare a snack; then she sits down on the couch and waits for her husband.

After a few minutes, she says, "Honey, the coffee is ready. Are you coming?"

He responds, "I'll be right there, dear. There was some laundry on the bed, and I'm putting it away."

After a few more minutes, she calls out, "Coffee is getting cold."

This time he answers, "Coming, dear! I was hanging up my tie and noticed that the light bulb had burned out. I'm going to change it for you."

After a few more minutes, she hears him in the kitchen and once again asks—now with an edge in her voice—"Are you coming now, dear?"

He responds, "I'm just throwing the old light bulb away."

When Dave finally gets to the couch, Ruth is getting up. "Just forget it. I'm sure you have something else to do!"

Dave is bewildered. What did he do? *I try to do so much to help her.*

Ruth's problem is not that her husband doesn't love her. He demonstrates his love through acts of service. But as wonderful as that is, he is not speaking her emotional love language.

Scenario Three

For twenty-five years, Betty begrudgingly accepted the many gifts her husband, Mike, bought for her. Time and time again she'd think, *This is frivolous. I don't need this.* Occasionally she caught a glimpse of hurt in Mike's face but dismissed it. After all, it was just a gift.

Later Betty learned about the five love languages and instantly recognized her husband's. She wept, realizing for the first time that she was rejecting her husband's expressions of love to her. What compounded her sorrow was learning that gift-giving was on the bottom of her list of love languages and that she rarely spoke that language to him—except at holidays. How discouraging it is to say "I love you," only to be rejected time and time again!

Betty learned the hard way that we must not only learn to speak the primary love language of our partners, but we must also learn to receive graciously all of their expressions of love.

Scenario Four

Gift-giving was last on the list of love languages for Kevin's mother and father, but it was at the top of his. His parents noticed that on each trip to the store, he consistently asked for money to buy something. For years, they interpreted his requests as an abnormal materialistic hang-up. Without success, they worked extra hard to break him of that trait.

When Kevin's parents learned about love languages, they realized that their son's primary love language was gift-giving. Equipped with a better understanding of their son, they tried a different approach. They started to bring home little gifts: a pack of gum, some pencils, a fancy eraser—nothing expensive, just little things intended to convey their love. That practice virtually eliminated his asking for things in the store. Mom and dad had learned to say "I love you" in a language their son could readily understand. If they hadn't, Kevin could have spent his teen years feeling unloved.

WHAT LANGUAGE DOES YOUR TEEN SPEAK?

As our last scenario indicates, it is just as important to learn your teen's primary love language as it is to learn your spouse's. Gift-giving is the primary love language of our youngest daughter. Many times we've arrived home and been greeted by Jennifer saying, "I made you a surprise." Whether she had baked a cake, pie, or cookies, she was saying "I love you" through gift-giving. In this case, she didn't give us something she had purchased; instead, she had given us a gift she had made herself as an act of love. In turn, we did the same for Jennifer and often gave her little gifts. A new hair ribbon would cause her face to light up because that little gesture confirmed in her heart our love for her.

Quality time is our eldest daughter's primary language. When we realized that, one of us would take Amy out for a leisurely lunch whenever possible. In so doing, we were saying "I love you" in a language she could easily understand. Moments of quality time happened throughout the week, too, but when we sat down at lunch and gave her undivided attention, love was confirmed in her heart.

Without some insight into primary love languages, it is easy for parents to misdiagnose a child's behavior and misjudge motives. This can result in frustrated parents and confused teens. We made the mistake ourselves.

After a weekend trip, we brought home stuffed bears for our children. When we gave one to Jennifer, she smooched and hugged us, saying, "Mom, Dad, thank you! This is wonderful. I love this little bear!"

Later we couldn't help commenting to each other, "That girl has such a thankful heart."

When we gave Amy her bear, she responded, "This is nice. Can I talk to you?"

"Come on, Amy," we pleaded. "Don't you want to arrange your new bear among all the others in your room?" After attempting to convince her of how wonderful the gift was, we turned to one another and concluded that Amy was not as thankful as Jennifer.

That was the wrong diagnosis! Amy was as thankful as Jennifer; we just misinterpreted her actions. Not understanding the dynamics of communicating love can be costly to a relationship. It is easy to misdiagnose a child's motives based on how we interpret his or her actions. That is why knowing a child's language of love is critical.

BIBLICAL LOVE

By now some of you might be wondering where 1 Corinthians 13 and other biblical teachings about love fit into the "languages" picture. God's call to love as He loved is what makes us choose to speak the other person's love language. Biblical love looks outward, not inward, yet at the same time, it satisfies all our inner needs.

In order for your teenagers to acknowledge the preciousness of others, they need to have learned a sense of love from you. Having a confirmed sense of love is not the basis for right behavior, but it does clear the way for a more comprehensive, proper love of others. One of the best ways to change a heart is to love a person when he or she is most unloving.

When biblical love is in the life of a teen, he or she will not be held back by the shackles of self-love, self-interest, and self-protection. The same is true of the parent. In that we all need to feel loved, we all remain children. That is why the family is so important. It should be a secure haven from which love flows. The ongoing demonstration of love between mom and dad should spill over to the children. Always remember: Every day we choose to love or not to love.

When we express love correctly in the context of the family, it makes it easier for each member to say "I love you" to those outside the family. When we love with a biblical love, we correctly represent God to the world.

QUESTIONS FOR REVIEW

Do you know each family member's love language? Here is an exercise for you and your teens to try. Rate each sentence on a scale of 1 to 5, according to what would make you feel most appreciated and loved by your spouse (or your parents or your teen). Five represents what you most appreciate; one, in contrast, is what you least appreciate. (Do not repeat a number within each group.) Please note that some questions distinguish between male and female. Answer those appropriately, according to your gender and position in the family.

GROUP ONE

A___Your spouse/teenager/parent says, "You really did a great job. I appreciate it."

B___Your spouse/teenager/parent unexpectedly does something in or around the house or your room that you appreciate.

C___Your spouse/teenager/parent brings you a surprise treat from the store.

D___Your spouse/teenager/parent invites you to go on a leisurely walk just to chat.

E___Your spouse/teenager/parent makes a point to embrace and kiss you before leaving the house.

GROUP TWO

A___Your spouse/teenager/parent tells you how much he or she appreciates you.

B___Your (male) spouse/teenager/parent volunteers to do the dishes and encourages you to relax. Your (female) spouse/teenager/parent volunteers to wash your car and encourages you to relax.

C___Your (male) spouse/teenager/parent brings you flowers, just because he cares. Your (female) spouse/teenager/parent brings you home a special treat from the local bakery.

D___Your spouse/teenager/parent invites you to sit down and talk about your day.

E___Your spouse/teenager/parent enjoys receiving a hug even when you're just passing from one room to another.

GROUP THREE

A___During a party your spouse/teenager/parent tells about one of your recent successes.

B___Your spouse/teenager/parent cleans out your car.

C___Your spouse/teenager/parent surprises you with an unexpected gift.

D___Your spouse/teenager/parent surprises you with a special afternoon trip.

E___Your spouse holds your hand as you walk through the mall, or your teenager/parent stands by your side with an arm around your shoulder at a public event.

GROUP FOUR

A___Your spouse/teenager/parent praises you about one of your special qualities.

B___Your spouse/teenager/parent brings you breakfast in bed.

C___Your spouse/teenager/parent surprises you with a membership to something you've always wanted.

D___Your spouse/teenager/parent plans a special night out for the two of you.

E___Your spouse/teenager/parent drives you to an event when you need a ride.

GROUP FIVE

A___Your spouse/teenager/parent tells you how much his or her friends appreciate you.

B___Your spouse/teenager/parent takes the time to fill out the long, complicated applications that you had hoped to find time for this evening.

C___Your spouse/teenager/parent sends you something special through the mail.

D___Your spouse/teenager/parent kidnaps you for lunch and takes you to your favorite restaurant.

E___Your spouse/teenager/parent gives you a massage.

SCORE SHEET

(Transfer your scores from your test questions to this scoring profile.)

Encouraging Words, Acts of Service, Gift Giving, Quality Time, Physical Touch and Closeness.

Group 1: A___B___C___D___E___
Group 2: A___B___C___D___E___

Group 3: A____B____C____D____E____
Group 4: A____B____C____D____E____
Group 5: A____B____C____D____E____

Totals: A____B____C____D____E____

Compare your score with your spouse/teenager/parent. List each family member's love languages, from the primary to the least important.

1._____

2._____

3._____

4._____

5._____

Now, purpose to speak each other's love language every day.

CHAPTER NINE

Why Teens Don't Talk or Listen

"When she was little, I couldn't even go to the bathroom without her talking to me through the door. Now she hardly says a word to me." The frustration and hurt in this mom's voice attest to the importance of good communication in family relationships.

Speaking and listening are God-given abilities that enable us to verbally express feelings. God understands our need for communication. He Himself is a communicating and conversational God. The Bible abounds with examples of God speaking to His people: He spoke to Adam and Eve in the garden, to the child Samuel in the Temple, and to Moses from a burning bush. The phrase "the Lord said" is used hundreds of times in the Bible.

Not only does God speak, but He also listens. He listens to the cries of His people and hears their prayers. He's not only the creator of communication, He's also the supreme example of its use.

In contrast, we can all improve our communication skills. We can listen more attentively and speak more graciously to one another, perhaps most of all to our teens. In this chapter, we will address common mistakes parents make in speaking and listening to their kids. This will set the stage for addressing the how-tos of improving two-way communication, which we will address in the following chapter.

PUTTING COMMUNICATION INTO PERSPECTIVE

It is important to note that improved communication will not cure all that is wrong in most struggling relationships. Communication has become a catchword in discussions about troubled marriages and struggling parents. While a lack of communication usually is a symptom of an unhealthy relationship, it is not necessarily true that the poor communication caused it.

Being a skilled communicator doesn't guarantee family harmony or healthy relationships. Communication skills are not a substitute for common or shared values. What holds families together is the moral unity found within the soul of the family. Moral intimacy among family members has no substitute, no backup, no replacement. Until we cultivate principle-centered relationships within our families, our efforts to improve communication will have little permanent value. Good speaking and listening skills are an important part of a healthy relationship, but they are not a substitute for it.

Knowing how to communicate with your spouse and kids is important, but even more important is learning how to biblically love and live with your family. Unconditional love not only should be the basis of our communication, it is the ultimate way we develop the rapport that characterizes healthy families.

Without Scripture's moral compass, our conversations can easily get turned around and lost in a wilderness called self. Communion of hearts and minds takes place between persons of like character. People who are morally like-minded get along better than people who are not.

WHY TEENS DON'T TALK

It doesn't take a professional counselor to figure out that good communication enhances relationships, while its poor counterpart signals relationship problems. Like the mother at the beginning of this chapter, we instinctively know something is wrong when our teens shut us out, but we don't always know what that something is. The best place to find our answer is from teens, so we surveyed a number of them. Like us, you may find their answers to be extremely enlightening. Below are the five reasons they gave for clamming up.

"My dad and mom don't talk to me."

Some parent-teen conversations never go beyond exchanging facts or giving instructions and correction. This is the lowest level of communication and occurs because parents are satisfied merely to receive or give data. This may be due to the busyness of the day, the rush to get dinner on the table, or the desire to head out the door for a meeting or event. But for whatever reason, parents sometimes don't pursue content in their conversations with their teens. Unfortunately, communication will not improve as long as the parent is satisfied to let it remain at this level.

Gathering facts pertaining to your child's day is important. Some small talk is necessary. But if that is the only level on which you communicate, don't be surprised if you get this type of exchange:

"How was your lunch today?"

"OK."

"How did you do on your quiz today?"

"I dunno."

"Where are you going tonight?"

"Out."

"Out where?"

"I dunno."

"Do you know when you're coming home?"

"Nope."

What is the cause of this sort of interchange? Which came first: the shallow conversation or the shallow relationship? We need to *really* talk to our kids—about matters of the heart—not just the mundane details of day-to-day existence. Healthy communication goes far beyond exchanging facts.

"My folks don't listen, anyway."

Sometimes kids get the impression that it is never the "right time" to talk with their parents or that they'll never get mom and dad's undivided attention during a conversation. Parents don't intend to send the message that they are unavailable or only half listening, but they frequently do. Preoccupation with jobs, chores, other kids, and even church can leave a teen feeling that everything else is more important than he or she is. Sharing dad or mom's attention with the newspaper, TV, computer, or grocery list is a put-off and a put-down.

There will be times when you can't talk "right now," but it's important to make time to do so whenever you can. During those times when you do talk, do you listen fully and with focused attention? Listening with your eyes is as much a part of the conversation as listening with your ears. If your eyes are watching your younger child or focusing out the window, you're only half listening. Teens become acutely aware of this. In such cases, not communicating at all produces less frustration for them than talking to a parent who only half listens.

"They answer before I even finish talking."

I, Gary, have failed my children this way on a number of occasions. Proverbs 18:13 says, "He who answers a matter before he hears it, it is folly and shame to him." There were times I thought I knew where a conversation was headed and jumped in with both feet, only to realize later that I had violated this proverb.

Like many parents, I had listened only long enough to get what I thought was the gist of what my child had to say and then quickly offered a solution: "OK, this is what you need to do."

One-half of my mind was listening; the other half was assessing the situation and deciding the solution.

Adolescents (and children) can quickly tell if you are really listening or are just surface listening, and they will respond accordingly. After all, would you want to keep talking with someone who rarely gave you the chance to speak your piece before hitting you with an ill-informed response? Probably not. Our teens don't like it either and will tend to avoid conversations of this sort. We need to focus on what our children are trying to say and let them say it before we offer a response.

"We never agree, anyway. So why talk?"

There may not be any cannons being shot, bullets zipping through the air, or covert sabotage taking place, but comments like this make it pretty obvious that the parent-teen relationship is in a state of cold war. In war, continual conflict shuts off healthy communication, and differences of opinion are perceived as threats.

In stress-filled families, conversations can quickly turn into arguments. As a result, both parent and child tend to pull away from each other, silently agreeing that it is preferable not to talk than to openly wage war.

Silence in the family is unnatural. It is a defense mechanism used not only by struggling parents and teens, but also by those in unhealthy marriages. To be silent is to be in control even when emotions are raging just below the surface. A point on our Family Reality Test in chapter 1 sums up the conversational low in many homes: "If it were not for sports or the weather, we probably wouldn't have anything safe to talk about to our teen." But even those topics can produce an argument in some families.

"There's nothing to talk to them about."

This condition is often the result of the independent family structure discussed in chapter 7. When family relationships are optional, talk is optional. The independent family structure affects communication in two ways.

First of all, the nature of independence breeds in-home isolation, not camaraderie. As a result, when there are problems or stress, the teens turn outward to their peers, not inward to their families. This is not only because peers are more available; in many cases, they are viewed as more credible.

Also the independent family fails to provide the opportunities that normally bring families together. Meals, bedtime, and family activities are regrouping times that allow for conversation. When you don't provide the environment for talk, talk doesn't happen.

WHY TEENS DON'T LISTEN

They hear the words of a new pop song, while we hear only the loud jumble of guitar chords and drumbeats. They listen for hours on the phone if we let them. And they catch the sound of a friend's car when it drives up. But sometimes our teenagers don't seem to hear one word we say.

Talking is only half the communication story. Many parents and teens talk to each other but don't always manage to communicate. There may be an exchange of words but not necessarily the sharing of information. Without someone hearing, reflecting, and responding to what is said, words mean little. Parents struggle in frustration when they feel their teens tune them out. Here's why some sons and daughters told us they do it.

"My folks don't do what they say, so why should I listen to them?"

"You're such a hypocrite!" This accusation usually triggers an immediate response from parents—anger, justification, or pain—often because there is some truth in the statement.

It is not easy to match our lives to our words, but that is the definition of integrity. Parents who don't live by the moral values they set up for the rest of the family are untrustworthy. The key word here is *moral*.

During the early years of childhood, parental authority may be challenged, but not parental integrity. Parents tell their children not to cross the street, light a fire, let the dog run loose, or climb daddy's ladder. Yet parents do these things without being perceived as hypocritical because these activities are not moral in nature. But when it comes to moral instruction and moral behavior, no disparity should exist between what parents teach and what they do. The moral rules the child is taught to live by are the same for the parent. Adulthood does not come with a new set of values. Moral truth does not vary with a person's age.

Teens use the moral standards taught to them by their parents to judge the behavior of friends, schoolmates, and teachers. It should not surprise us, then, when our teens use those same standards to judge us.

"I've already heard it a dozen times."

Nothing makes a teen tune out faster than constantly "reminding" him or her of faults or responsibilities. Homework and chores are often a case in point. Frequently no ground rules are established, or if they are, they are not enforced. That leaves mom and dad repeatedly saying things such as "Have you finished your homework? Your math grade is slipping. You need to discipline yourself. This is your responsibility...."

By the third "lecture," teens do know what their parents are going to say even if they phrase it differently, so kids stop listening. Overtalk is communication overkill. We need to communicate effectively in order to teach the values governing personal responsibility, but harping or nagging is not effective communication.

"My parents are sarcastic. They just put me down."

In an effort to draw attention to their teens' behavior problems, some parents use sarcasm in their daily conversation as a
tool of coercion. Listen for the verbal barbs. "Of course you eat
healthy enough. Those potato chips are a vegetable." "So, what
kind of trouble did you get into at school today?" "When you act
that way, I'm surprised you have any friends at all."

It's difficult to get teens or anyone, for that matter, to listen
when they are treated disrespectfully. Teens don't forget put-
downs. Turnoff words and put-down phrases force one of two
reactions from teens. Either they verbally attack the source of irri-
tation with their own sarcasm, or they withdraw in silence. In
both cases, the results are the same—the teens stop listening.

Some parents use sarcasm because they think it will help
motivate their kids, but teens resist this type of "motivation" and
become cynical of anything the parent says. This has a downward-
spiraling effect. The parent's new efforts to make amends are seen
as just another twisted effort to control, rather than build the relationship. So the teen tunes out in revenge. To tune out is to take
control.

"I know just as much as my mom and dad do."

Teens can sense when parents are unsure of their own beliefs
or leadership decisions. This doesn't mean a parent can't say, "I'm
not sure how to answer you. I need time to think it through." But
it does mean that once the decision is made, parents know their
reasons and stick to them.

Too often we get into the habit of making decisions without
thinking them through. Then we start waffling, "Well, maybe this
time…." When this happens repeatedly, teens tend to acknowledge the parents' instructions, but they do what they please. They
stop listening because they don't believe their parents are sure of
what they are saying or that they have the resolve to enforce it.
This teen has greater confidence in his own ability to make deci-

sions than in his parents'. He or she becomes "wise in his own eyes" (Proverbs 26:12).

When a parent says, "If you do this, such and such will happen," but it doesn't happen due to lack of parental resolve or failure to follow through, it causes the teen to further become wise in his own eyes. Before your teen will listen and follow your instructions, he or she needs to know you believe your own words.

"My parents don't expect me to listen."

Parents sometimes expect too little out of their relationship with their teen. They think it's normal for teenagers to be in constant conflict with them and that not talking and not listening are inevitable parts of adolescent behavior.

As we mentioned earlier, our society expects teens to resist parental leadership and defy any infringement on their autonomy. Instead of promoting the idea that we can have great relationships with our teenage sons and daughters, we are faced with a nightmarish stereotype of parents pitted against teens in a lose-lose contest of wills.

Adopting any or all of society's expectations affects our parenting. We set rules and say things based more on a stereotype than on who our teen actually is. This can't help but cause him or her to neither talk to us nor listen to what we say. And the more powerless we feel to direct our children's lives, the greater our tendency is to control rather than to lead. So the relational cycle spirals downward to the point where there is no talking and no listening.

However, the reverse can also be true. Tuning in to the true nature of our teens can promote talking and listening. When you truly get to know someone and expect his or her best, your efforts on that person's behalf make you safe to talk with and credible to listen to.

This concludes our study of the common mistakes we parents make in talking with our teens. Now let's look at ways of improving two-way communication.

QUESTIONS FOR REVIEW

1. Why is good communication not a guarantee of strong family relationships?

2. Look up Proverbs 18:13, and write the communication principle it states.

3. List the things that you and your teenager can talk about.

4. Of the five reasons teens don't listen to their parents, which one do you struggle with the most? Which is not a problem for you?

CHAPTER TEN

Mouth and Ear Coordination

Not long ago, we asked a young woman who'd just celebrated her twentieth birthday why she hadn't rebelled during her teen years. Put on the spot, she said, "I think for me, it came down to trusting what my mom and dad said and knowing they listened to what I said."

Healthy, proactive communication is one of the best forms of adolescent encouragement. Good communication can prevent more conflicts than corrections can solve.

A teen's vocabulary and self-understanding are more mature than a child's. Teens are now able to more readily express inner, abstract feelings. This makes adolescence an opportunity for meaningful talk. You can learn how to talk so your kids will listen, and you can learn to listen so your kids will talk.

Communication allows us to transfer thoughts, emotions, feelings, and ideas, but it doesn't just happen. We must work to perfect the skills that will bring legitimacy to our words and will cause our teens to listen to us.

GOD'S GUIDELINES

The first priority of open and honest communication with our teens is to create and maintain a climate of trust so they feel secure enough to talk. This involves submitting ourselves to the biblical ethics governing how we speak and listen.

COMMUNICATION ETHICS

For Speaking:

- "A soft answer turns away wrath, but a harsh word stirs up anger." Proverbs 15:1
- "The wise in heart will be called prudent, and sweetness of the lips increases learning." Proverbs 16:21
- "A word fitly spoken is like apples of gold," and "Like one who takes away a garment in cold weather, and like vinegar on soda, is one who sings songs to a heavy heart." Proverbs 25:11a, 20
- "Pleasant words are like a honeycomb, sweetness to the soul and health to the bones." Proverbs 16:24
- "Let your speech always be with grace, seasoned with salt, that you may know how you ought to answer each one." Colossians 4:6

For Listening:

- "He who answers a matter before he hears it, it is folly and shame to him." Proverbs 18:13
- "The first one to plead his cause seems right, until his neighbor comes and examines him." Proverbs 18:17
- "But who ever listens to me will dwell safely, and will be secure, without fear of evil." Proverbs 1:33
- "Let every man be swift to hear, slow to speak, slow to wrath." James 1:19

Proverbs 15:1 addresses the tone of our words: "A soft answer turns away wrath, but harsh words stir up anger." Colossians 4:6 encourages us to employ well-chosen words: "Let your speech always be with grace, seasoned with salt, that you may know how you ought to answer each one." The ethics of Scripture also govern listening. Proverbs 18:17 teaches us not to listen to just one side of the story: "The first one to plead his cause seems right, until his neighbor comes and examines him." James 1:19 tells us, "Let every man be swift to hear, slow to speak, and slow to wrath." None of us will master all of these principles all of the time. But these communication guidelines are from God and therefore must be followed to the best of our abilities.

There's a tendency to think that God's ethics are good ideals but impossible to practice consistently. But everything in life is learned; just because we fail from time to time, that doesn't mean we cease striving to make God's ethics the cornerstone of all our relationships.

DEEPER MOMENTS

When our kids were growing up, the primary times for talking in the Ezzo household were at dinner and bedtime. When our kids were younger, we talked more at dinner than at bedtime. But when they were teens, we talked more at bedtime than at any other time. We had an interesting arrangement. Some nights the girls sat on the edge of our bed, tucking us in while recounting the day's activities. The next night it was our turn to sit on the edge of their beds and talk.

This accomplished more than simply providing an extended time to talk. It provided a necessary opportunity to care for our family at a deeper level of communion. All those nights spent sitting on each other's beds, listening to one another, and participating in meaningful conversation, ministered to each of us at a deeper level than could be achieved at most other times. We interacted and tried to empathize with each other. We connected to each other at a deeper level than when we talked about dad's day at work or the kids' day at school.

This is a powerful experience. The deep impression of the

family residing in each other's heart united us in ways that no principle alone can explain. Just as our communion with Jesus Christ is not merely appreciation for the ink and type on the pages of the Bible but is instead a deep and abiding relationship, so also is this dynamic, expressed as the talking soul of the family. When talk-time didn't take place for one reason or another, there was much discontent and loneliness among our family members.

Some families do not know what they don't have. They don't realize the value of time—of using their special moments to develop the soul of the family—until they no longer have it.

THE TEN-TALK RULE

One of the great hindrances to communication is time. Sometimes we just can't stop and talk and give our full attention when our children ask for it. Sometimes they just want to talk, and other times they need to talk—right now. How do we find the right balance between meeting their immediate needs and staying focused on the project in front of us, which may equally need our attention?

To find that balance in our family, we used the "ten-talk rule." It was a privilege and a trust to invoke this rule. If our children absolutely and immediately needed our attention, they'd say, "Dad, I need to talk with you, and this is a ten-talk."

Using a scale of one to ten, ten being most urgent, our children were trusted to grade their own need and tell us. A grade between one and five meant, "I want to talk with you"; between six and ten, it meant, "I need to talk with you."

The ten-talk privilege was taken seriously. It meant we were going to trust our children to assess the urgency of their need in light of our present activities. For example, Gary was less flexible with his time when working on a Sunday message than when he was reading a Western novel.

THE EZZO TALK SCALE

Ten Talk: "This is most urgent; I need to talk right now, Dad."
Eight Talk: "This is urgent. Can you give me some time in the next hour?"
Six Talk: "As soon as you're done, Dad, we need to talk. Even if it means later tonight."
Four Talk: "Dad, when you find some time for me today, tonight, or tomorrow, I would like to talk with you."
Two Talk: "Dad, get back to me sometime. I have some questions to ask you."

Before coming into Dad's office and evoking the ten-talk rule, our children gave plenty of thought to what they were asking. Could it wait a few minutes, hours, or even days? Could mom answer the question? Our kids knew we trusted them with the privilege of their own assessment. They also knew that we could be trusted to listen attentively and completely when they really needed it. That mutual trust further served to build our healthy communication.

Did they make judgmental errors? Yes, of course they did. But they learned from their mistakes and became more discerning.

CONTENT VS. INTENT

In the 1970s, comedian Flip Wilson popularized the phrase "Read my lips." Parents need to do more than read their kids' lips; they need to read their hearts. Healthy communication requires that parents listen to what is being felt as much as what is actually being said.

Try to understand the message of your teen's heart. Not to do so, in effect, rejects your child. We play a dangerous and destructive game if we routinely fail to listen for feelings.

On one occasion, our daughter Amy shared that she had no

close friends. Off the cuff, Gary responded, "Of course you do. Don't be silly!" Although he was trying to sound encouraging, he actually cut her communication short. He listened to her words but not to her feelings. Later that evening, Anne Marie informed Gary of a struggle Amy was having with a close friend. In this case, Anne Marie had responded by listening to the deeper message. She listened between the lines rather than reacting only to the words on the surface.

When listening for the unspoken message, concentrate on the way your son or daughter is speaking—the body language, facial expression, tone of voice, and sense of urgency being conveyed. Parents gain greater insights, knowledge, and sensitivity when they listen to nonverbal messages.

The benefits are enormous. Teens respond positively and grow in their confidence that you care about what they feel and think. In-depth listening gives your children the respect they deserve and sets the standard of respect and focused attention that you require of them when it is your turn to talk.

EXPRESS VS. VENT

Allowing teens to express their feelings properly is a vital part of good communication. But some people minimize their expression of emotions while others exaggerate them. Emotional displays, either minimized or exaggerated, impact the person receiving them. To mask your feelings is to deny you have them, but to vent them openly without a care for others can lead to painful resentment by everyone involved.

People send emotional signals at every encounter. The closer they are to someone, the more their true feelings leak out. Thus, they are more likely to vent, rather than express their feelings to their families. We have a communications covenant in our family: We will not stop loving each other in moments when feelings of frustration, hostility, and anger escape from us.

Healthy families know the difference between expressing feelings and venting them. Sure, there will be days when someone in the family is in a bad mood, uncommunicative, and generally unpleasant to live with. Bad days and good days visit all of us because we are human. But how are you generally characterized? How do you respond when you're angry or upset? Are you able to let the rest of the family know what you feel without saying something you'll regret later?

There is a big difference between honestly expressing your feelings and the more explosive method of doing so—venting. Expressing feelings reflects the present state of affairs which may be quite unpleasant, and this is understandable. But venting tends to be exaggerated, explosive, often nonsensical, and belligerent.

The practice of ventilation therapy came from the writings of Freud and was carried forward by his disciples. Parents are warned that a child's psychological health depends on his ability to vent his hostilities and anger and to be verbally aggressive when needed, even to the point of verbal abuse. The theory didn't work for Freud, and it doesn't work with children. Furthermore, it doesn't aid healthy communication. We are not implying that a child should not be allowed to share his or her feelings. We are simply stating that these must be expressed in a socially and morally acceptable manner. No self-help is derived from an out-of-control experience. We've all been there before. It's neither pleasant nor God-honoring.

We must all manage our exchange of emotions—not prevent, but manage them. Teens should have the freedom to express their feelings and have them acknowledged by their parents. Parents should have the same freedom. In both cases, self-control must be exercised. It helps to set family guidelines beforehand.

EMPATHY: COMMUNICATION'S HEART

One day our daughter came home from high school. Gary knew something was wrong by the look on her face and the droop of her shoulders. He risked an exploratory statement. "Jen, you look like you're hurting. It's obvious that it hasn't been a good day. I'm sorry about that."

She gave him a half-hearted smile and said, "It's nothing, Dad."

Gary decided not to pry into her private world. He remembered being put off more than once by someone asking, "Do you want to talk about it?" Sometimes we need to choose with whom and when we share troubles. His statement let her know that he cared.

Later that afternoon, Gary was weeding his garden when Jenny came outside, pulled up a crate, and sat down. She started talking about Martha, a new girl she had befriended. Apparently Martha had also become friends with Jenny's best friend, Sarah. Suddenly Jenny was no longer included in Martha and Sarah's plans. She had been nudged out and made a third wheel. It hurt.

GUIDELINES FOR EXPRESSING FEELINGS

- When upset, you may speak faster than normal, but you must speak clearly.
- You may talk louder than usual, but you can't shout.
- You can feel anger, but may not act on it.
- You can go to your room to get control, but you cannot stomp your feet on the way there.
- You can punch your pillow, but you cannot slam your door.
- You can tell your parents you believe they are wrong, but you cannot dishonor them.
- You can tell your children what's wrong with their behavior, but you cannot attack their dignity as a person by calling them names or belittling them.

Jennifer asked, "Why, Dad, after all these years of being best friends, would Sarah just drop me like that? Sarah wears Martha's clothes and her jewelry and goes home with her after school. And she has only known her for a couple of weeks."

"It hurts to watch your best friend take off with the new kid, especially the kid you introduced her to," Gary responded. Jenny was curious. It never occurred to her that one of her parents might have lost a best friend in a similar manner. Gary began to reflect on an incident from his own youth.

Afterward Jenny asked, "What do you think I should do?"

"Wait, I guess. Give it some time. Don't try to force yourself into the relationship by playing games. That will only rob you of your integrity. Be gracious with Sarah; maybe she will see that real friendships can never be bought with fancy clothes and expensive jewelry. If you and Sarah were really best friends, she'll come back. Real friendships are not forgotten."

For a teen struggling with life, there is no more important resource than a parent with a capacity for empathy. Letting our kids know that we understand what they are feeling because we have been there ourselves serves to tighten the relational ties. It is a concrete way for them to know we truly do understand.

Incidentally, a week later Jennifer came waltzing into Gary's office after school. She wore a smile that lit up the room. She looked at him and with a twinkle in her eye said, "Dad, Sarah wrote me a note today and apologized for being such a jerk. She told me how foolish she had been to think that all of Martha's beautiful clothes and flashy jewelry could ever replace me. She wants us to be best friends as we always have been."

Gary hugged her. Jenny whispered, "Thanks, Dad; you were right. I waited, and she came back."

We've lost track of how many times since then that Jenny and Amy have asked one of us, "Did you ever go through something like this?" Empathy breeds confidence in parental counsel. Share yourself with your kids. Share your failures and your successes, your own adolescent hurts and pains. Tell them the stories of your childhood struggles. We all had them. When teens awaken to the fact that "there is nothing new under the sun" and that every generation experiences similar relational testing and trials, they tend to turn to parents with renewed confidence.

We should add that sharing our past with our kids doesn't mean we must disclose deep personal information. Past sinful lifestyles are best kept where God put them: "As far as the east is from the west, so far has He removed our transgressions from us" (Psalm 103:12). Revealing without discretion may be unwise and even corrupting. But sharing to communicate empathy can make a big difference in parent-teen communication.

QUESTIONS FOR REVIEW

1. Which biblical ethics of either talking or listening do you feel parents most commonly violate? Which ones do you need to work on?

2. List a couple of times in your family day that could be used for opportunities for deeper talk. Choose one possibility, and plan how you will use it to reach out to your teen this week.

3. As the parent and the example, think about how you handle your feelings. Do you bury, vent, or express them? How can you improve?

4. Think about this last week with your teen. Describe a time you used or could have used empathy to encourage communication. Look for opportunities to do so in the following week.

PART IV

MAINTAING HEARTS

CHAPTER ELEVEN

How to Say How

A strong will and an emotional nature made Carol's fourteen-year-old daughter, Lisa, a handful. She responded dramatically to most requests and directives. Initially Carol reacted to Lisa's behavior, but the resulting conflict caused her to do some serious thinking. She started to take note of what defused and what exploded each situation. She even began to see a correlation between Lisa's responses and her own methods of instruction.

Over time, Carol learned that Lisa did much better when directives and consequences were discussed before problems arose. To her relief, she also found that by changing her own communication style, she was able to reduce the amount of conflict in her relationship with her daughter.

THE STARTING POINT

As we discussed in earlier chapters, developing healthy patterns of communication is basic to healthy parenting. The next principle we want to share is that learning to communicate instructions to our children is also essential to proper parenting. This is because instruction is the starting point of all moral training. In the preceding example, Carol thought that she was instructing her daughter. But when she took the time to think through their relationship, Carol realized that she was *reacting to and arguing* with her child rather than *instructing* her. Learning how to instruct, to coach from the sidelines of your child's life, is essential to a strong parent-teen relationship, but it takes a conscious effort.

The burden of instruction may seem overwhelming to many parents. However, we are not on our own in training our children in morality. Scripture provides us with the guidelines we need. When Solomon penned the book of Proverbs, he referred to instruction directly and indirectly more than one hundred times. He connects instruction with wisdom, right and just living, child training and correction, fool prevention, and a parent's future delight. Clearly and repeatedly, history's wisest man establishes instruction as the starting point for moral training.

"Fools despise wisdom and instruction," Solomon warns in Proverbs 1:7. But "correct your son, and he will give you rest; yes, he will give delight to your soul" (Proverbs 29:17). In this context, the word *correct* means to educate your child. As used here, it doesn't mean to punish, but to train. Proverbs 22:6 tells us to "train up a child in the way he should go, and when he is old he will not depart from it." Here the word *train* means to initiate learning, to set the patterns of learning, and to cause one to learn. Proverbs 19:18 says, "Chasten your son while there is hope, and do not set your heart on his destruction." The message is clear: If your teen is going to learn, it is your job as a parent to instruct.

MORAL INSTRUCTION AND EXAMPLE

To avoid confusion, we must clarify the difference between moral instruction and general rules. Stealing and lying are immoral acts. They are equally wrong for parent and teen. In contrast, a ten o'clock bedtime is not a moral obligation but a health consideration. This requirement is for the youth, not necessarily for the parent.

This contrast should heighten your awareness of the importance of being a moral example to your children at all ages. Parental example must support parental instruction. Instruction without example is authoritarian and produces a teen who is bitter and full of resentment. Example without teaching is permissive and produces a teen who is exasperated, insecure, and left to himself morally. Thus, that which is morally right for the teen must also be morally right for the parent.

Parents should train their children by instruction, but not all instruction will be of the classroom variety. We all learn from simple commands which are either directive (telling us what to do) or restrictive (telling us what not to do). It is because we are often unaware of these differences that problems and conflicts develop.

As a parent, listen to the type of instruction you give. Are you the type who only gives commands? Or worse, do you tend to be the permissive type who never gives any? Do your instructions teach the intellect but not the heart? Do you demand new tasks of your teen without showing him or her how to do them?

Most methods of instruction have value, and they fulfill a learning purpose. There is a time and a place for each method, and all are usually best accomplished during periods of peace. Moses spoke of this in Deuteronomy 6:6–9 when he said, "These words which I command you today shall be in your heart." Literally, this phrase can be read "as a weight on your heart," implying a sense of urgency. In verses 7 through 9, Moses instructs parents to teach their children diligently and to do it during the course of daily activities. The word *teach* implies structured instruction. Parents do not merely assist in a child's learning process. When a child is ready to learn, it is mom and dad's responsibility to teach.

The type of teaching spoken of by Moses is not corrective nor punitive, but admonishing and encouraging. It is wise teaching directed toward the child while he is standing, sitting, walking, or lying down. We instruct by correcting, admonishing, warning, rebuking, and encouraging. In essence, we are to continually teach our children all we know about life.

A POINT OF CONFLICT

Learning how to effectively communicate instructions to our children is essential to proper parenting—and to avoiding problems. Many parent-teen conflicts start at the point of instruction. When we consider the vital role of instruction in a teen's life, there are a few facts and elementary principles to keep in mind. Following these basic guidelines can prevent stress and increase willing compliance; failure to comply can lead to power struggles and outright rebellion.

Principle One: To Ask or to Tell

When giving instructions, be sure to say exactly what you mean and mean precisely what you say. Parents commonly violate this simple principle. There is no better way to teach a teen not to obey than to give instructions you have no intention of enforcing or to make requests that are in reality veiled orders.

By telling your teen, "Take out the trash," you are communicating that you have an expectation he or she must meet. If a failure to obey is not met with consequences, your teen quickly learns that obedience is optional. This conclusion is sure to lead to frustration—both for you and your child—and almost certainly conflict.

On the other hand, if you ask your teen, "Would you mind taking out the trash?" you are making a request. In the face of options—taking out the trash or *not* taking out the trash—your teen may choose to leave the garbage in its current position under the kitchen sink. Your expression of disapproval at this point sends mixed messages. Your teen realizes that the options presented were not truly options. Your request was a test...and he or she failed. This situation leads to misunderstanding and mistrust...and once again, conflict.

In the absence of parental resolve, a teen quickly learns the habit of disregarding all requests. Ultimately, this habit can become so strong and contempt for instruction so confirmed that all threats will go unheeded. Both directive instructions and restrictive instructions require a response of immediate obedience unless otherwise stated in the instructions.

Principle Two: Now or When?

Parents should consider the timing of their instructions. Sometimes timing is as important as the instruction itself. Parental instruction that interrupts or terminates an activity should often be preceded by a warning such as "You need to finish up in five minutes. I want you to...."

We all know what it's like to become absorbed in a project, and we know the frustration of having to set aside our efforts without warning. Teens feel this same frustration. A five-minute warning indicates that instruction requiring compliance will soon be coming. Such a benevolent act helps a teen (or any of us, for that matter) to emotionally prepare to stop what he or she is doing and be ready to comply. Parental sensitivity of this sort reduces the shock of intrusion and alleviates the tension between the child's desire to continue with an activity and the need to comply with his parent's instruction.

Principle Three: If, Ands, or Buts

Parents should allow for an appeal process. Many times we give instructions to our kids but are not fully aware of the context in which we've given our instructions. Sometimes they create unnecessary exasperation in our children. When we allow an appeal process, our teens have an acceptable, respectful way to handle their frustration.

A POINT OF APPEAL

Examples of appealing to authority can be found in both the Old and New Testaments. The first chapter of Daniel tells of the young prophet and his three friends who were slaves in King Nebuchadnezzar's court. Their position called for them to eat food forbidden by the law of Moses. When Daniel made up his mind not to defile himself by eating the king's food, he appealed to the commander of the officials. Daniel's appeal won him the favor of his captors.

THE BENEFITS OF APPEAL

Like all Bible-based principles, the appeal process has many benefits. They are not only for parents and teens but also families and society. Below are some of the ones we realized while raising our daughters.

- It makes obedience more attractive since the teen knows his or her parents are approachable and willing to revisit previously given instruction.
- It protects teens from becoming needlessly frustrated.
- It prepares teens to interact correctly with present and future authorities.
- It prevents parental authority from being arbitrary, legalistic, or authoritarian.
- It allows parents the right to change their minds without the fear of compromising their authority.
- It encourages sibling relationships as each child learns to appeal to the others.
- It reinforces family harmony during the teen years. When children grow confident of their parents' fairness, the harmony derived is further magnified in the teen years.

In the New Testament, the apostle Paul appealed to Caesar (Acts 25:11). Later, in the book of Philemon, he appealed to the owner of a runaway slave to forgive and receive the offender. Clearly there is a biblical precedent for appealing to authority.

Both authoritarian and permissive parents have difficulty with the appeal process. That is because the authoritarian parent sees authority as absolute, regardless of parental error or misjudgment. The permissive parent, on the other hand, rejects the role of authority altogether and, therefore, has no use for its safeguards.

For those standing between these extremes, the appeal process can help bring authority into focus. To appeal to authority is to acknowledge another's rule in our lives. To be in a position of leadership and to hear an appeal is to accept our human imperfection. Remember, none of us is a perfect parent. We all make errors in judgment. Thankfully, God in his graciousness has provided principles that can help us build strong relationships with our teens in spite of our shortcomings.

THE NEED

Colossians 3:20–21 speaks to the issue of children and obedience. In the same passage, Paul warns against provoking and discouraging children. The fact is, the very nature of required compliance will often frustrate a teenager, but that does not mean we do away with the standards of acceptable behavior or common courtesies. So how do parents achieve the necessary balance in maintaining order in the home without exasperating their teens? The answer is found in the appeal process.

Discernment dictates that a parent not ask a teen to turn off the television right before a show ends. Nor would a discerning parent ask a teen to put away a computer game if it were near completion. Those are the types of actions that unnecessarily frustrate teens and violate the principle of not provoking our children. Yet, all of us are insensitive at times, act without understanding the situation, or act from a different point of reference. This is why the appeal process is necessary.

With the appeal process, the teen becomes proactive in providing *new information* that will help the parent make an informed decision about his or her previous instruction. "Mom, I don't want to" is not new information. That is a preference. The appeal process alerts a parent to a different reference point—that of the child.

Caleb was watching an auto-racing video that was within five minutes of ending. His mom didn't realize how close it was to the end and told her son to turn off the television and wash up for dinner. In this case, her frame of reference was dinner, which was about to be placed on the table. Caleb's frame of reference was the

---

APPEAL GUIDELINES

To avoid problems in the appeal process, consider the following guidelines.

1. The appeal must only be made to the parent giving the instructions, otherwise it undermines the authority of both parents.

2. Parents should entertain an appeal only when the child comes in humility. A gentle spirit communicates a child's recognition of his parents' right to rule and overrule.

3. The teen must appeal with new information to help the parent understand the context of the situation which is the subject of the teen's appeal. This process should not be used to create a forum to state likes and dislikes.

4. If the appeal process is to work effectively, parents must be fair and flexible. Think about why you say "no." Is there a good reason it cannot sometimes be "yes"?

video, which was near completion. As a result of her request, tension was created. Should Caleb comply but be frustrated? Or should he risk ignoring his mother in order to satisfy his desire to watch the race's conclusion? Compliance would leave Caleb in a state of exasperation, and his mother would have unknowingly violated Colossians 3:21. Yet if he took a chance and ignored her instruction, his disobedience would violate Colossians 3:20. Either way, there is cause for parent-teen conflict. The appeal process bridges the two verses, preventing disobedience and, equally important, preventing exasperation.

WHEN AND HOW?

To activate an appeal, the teen, not the parent, must initiate the process by providing new information. The parent's job is to hear and to act on that information, realizing that "yes," "no," and "maybe" are all possible answers.

Providing a personal opinion is not the same thing as providing new information. Many children offer a commentary, an analysis, or an opinion on parental instruction. However, that is not providing new, factual information which forms the basis of a legitimate appeal.

In Caleb's case, he should appeal his mom's instruction by saying, "Mom, there are only five minutes left on the video. May I finish it first?" With new information, his mom may reconsider the request without compromising her leadership.

His appeal is legitimate, and there is probably no reason his mother would not change her mind and say, "Yes, that's fine. When it is over, please wash up for dinner." Now everyone wins. There is no exasperation, no conflict, and no power struggle. Without the appeal process, problems develop easily.

Bob and his family found seats together at a ballgame, but Christopher, age twelve, sat several seats away. When Bob

---

TEACHING THE APPEAL PROCESS

1. Sit down with your teen and work through the appeal process and its guidelines.

2. Set up a few scenarios that might fit your family situation. Include in each one an example of how to correctly and incorrectly make an appeal.

3. Once your teens master the concepts, allow the natural consequences of their choices to reinforce your training. If they come to you with a wrong attitude or if they fail to bring new information, deny their appeal. If they start to appeal everything, take the privilege away for several weeks.

---

instructed him to move closer, Christopher responded, "No, Dad, I want to sit here!" Christopher's answer challenged authority and created conflict. If Bob repeated himself, he would reinforce Christopher's noncompliance. If he gave in, he would be compromising his authority and parental integrity. The "no" response forced Bob to take corrective measures.

After receiving a verbal admonishment, Christopher explained his frame of reference. "Dad, I sat over there because I couldn't see all the players with that banner hanging so low." Was that a legitimate reason to sit away from the family? Yes. Was it handled the best way? No. An appeal by Christopher could have prevented the entire scene.

Remember, the appeal process is built on trust. The teen trusts the parent to be fair and flexible, and the parent trusts the child to bring new information that legitimizes the appeal process.

The appeal process is not a cute trick to avoid conflict. Rather, it helps develop a lifelong character-building trait. The willingness of an individual to submit to authority is directly related to the fairness exhibited by that authority. In general, life is not fair. Yet parents can be fair without compromising their authority by teaching their children how to approach them with reasonable appeals.

QUESTIONS FOR REVIEW

1. Why do you think Solomon connected instruction with wisdom—a parent's future delight?

2. How can giving your teen a five-minute warning that instructions will follow prevent exasperation?

3. Think about what you want your teen to do tomorrow. Write down how to say what you really mean. Should it be worded as a request or a command? When would be a good time to state it?

4. List advantages of the appeal process for your family. What are the disadvantages?

5. Think about the last month, and write down an incident in which the appeal process would have benefited the situation.

CHAPTER TWELVE

A Word of Encouragement

The hassle wasn't new. Becky expected her teenage daughter's room to be picked up each morning. Yet when she went past the open door to Donna's room one afternoon, yesterday's clothes, towel, and books dotted the floor and bed. Confronting her daughter later, Becky told her, "You know your room needs to be picked up in the morning. Since you didn't do it then, you can do it now, along with the bathroom."

After finishing the work, Donna asked to talk. "My room is clean, Mom, but I really feel upset. I kept it picked up all week, and you never said one word. Then the one day I don't get it done, you get on my case. You seem to notice only the bad things I do."

THE BASICS OF BIBLICAL DISCIPLINE

At some point Becky undoubtedly asked herself or others, "How should I handle this messy-bedroom problem?" There seems to be a prevailing assumption that if parents can master better methods of punishment, they'll solve their parent-teen conflicts. Surely punishment plays a role in child-training, but in the teen years, it should play a greatly diminished role. Unfortunately, as the story of Becky and Donna illustrates, more effective solutions—such as encouragement or natural and logical consequences—are often missed.

Fundamental to the process of encouragement and punishment is a basic understanding of the term *discipline*. Let's begin by defining the word. Most parents think only of punishment when they think of discipline, but discipline is simply a process of training and learning that fosters moral development. It comes from the same root word as *disciple*, which means *one who is a learner*. The purpose of discipline is to teach morally responsible behavior; it is therefore critical that parents understand the basics of biblical discipline. The positive aspects of biblical discipline are synonymous with education and guidance in that they emphasize inner growth, personal responsibility, and self-control. All of these qualities lead to behavior motivated from within one's heart (Proverbs 4:23).

God's purpose for discipline is precise. It is to bring about the peaceful fruit of righteousness. Hebrews 12:11 states, "Now no chastening seems to be joyful for the present, but grievous; nevertheless, afterward it yields the peaceable fruit of righteousness to those who have been trained by it."

Biblical discipline consists of a number of essential principles and actions, some encouraging, some corrective. Various forms of encouragement that complement the biblical process include affirmation, goal incentives, praise, and rewards. The corrective side consists of verbal reproof, natural consequences, isolation, restrictions, loss of privileges, and chastisement. Each activity has purpose, meaning, and a legitimate place in the overall process.

DISCIPLINING MORAL AND NONMORAL BEHAVIOR

Before we get into the specific actions and principles of discipline, it is important to revisit the fact that behavior falls into two categories, moral and nonmoral (or amoral). Learning to swim, tie a shoelace, ride a bike, kick a ball, climb a rope, play the piano, or memorize the multiplication tables are nonmoral activities. They are skills associated with natural gifts, talents, and mental attributes.

They are functions of life, but not matters of morality.

In contrast, obedience, kindness, honesty, respect, honor, and integrity are the beginning of a long list of moral attributes. Parents need to remain mindful of the difference between moral and morally neutral behavior. Why? Because the encouragement and correction process for developing a personal skill differs from the encouragement and correction process of modifying behavior. The first focuses on a child's natural abilities; the second on his or her heart.

Learning to ride a bike is a skill, but riding a bike in such a way as not to hurt someone is behavioral. Not knowing how to swim is an unlearned skill, but bullying other children in the water is wayward behavior. It's wrong to treat these equally. One is related to deficiencies in skills, while the other is a moral weakness.

Encouraging Nonmoral Behavior

There are three essential elements required in the development of skills: patience, guidance, and motivation. For a child to be willing to invest time and effort in the practice needed to develop a skill, there must be some source of motivation. Parents can help in this area by praise and goal incentives. Often verbal praise goes a long way. It can make a difference to say something as simple as "Your game has improved a lot, Jeremy, ever since you added ten minutes to your practice time."

These words link encouragement to the cause and effect of your teen's efforts. Tying your encouragement to a specific activity helps the child to measure the value of his practice and encourages him or her to continue putting forth effort.

Encouraging Moral Behavior

Moral behavior is associated with the heart. Parents motivate the heart by encouragement and correction. Both activities are important, and neither one is truly effective without the other. In this chapter we will concentrate on encouragement; in chapter 13 we will tackle the how-tos of correction.

THE EXTRA MILE

When you encourage your teen in the context of a biblical relationship, you are offering a powerful motivator for right behavior. Outside that context, however, encouraging words can sound hypocritical. The comments of a father who does not take the time to establish a trusting relationship with his son or daughter are meaningless. Hearing an encouraging word is not the same as having an encouraging parent.

Unfortunately, this is an area in which many parents fail, particularly during the teen years. During this time, parents are so preoccupied with getting things under control by continually

---

AN ENCOURAGEMENT POLL

We asked one hundred teens between ninth and twelfth grade to list for us what their parents do or say that encourages them most. Here are the top five responses in order of their ranking.

1. Teens feel motivated to do right when they have a sense that their parents trust them.

2. Teens feel motivated to do right when they feel respected by their parents. That is, encouragement works better than put-downs.

3. Teens feel motivated to do right when their parents live the standard they are being asked to live.

4. Teens feel motivated to do right when they are given the moral reasons why.

5. Teens feel motivated to do right when parents are willing to acknowledge their own mistakes, instead of making up excuses.

correcting, they generally forget to encourage. And as we all know from personal experience, the absence of encouragement is the same thing as discouragement.

There are a number of ways to encourage teens. Remember the five love languages we talked about in chapter 8? Verbal praise, physical touch, simple gifts, spending time together, acts of service—each expression of love sends the message that we notice what our kids do and we care about them. But encouragement doesn't just happen. No matter which form of it we use, we must take the time to really notice behavior and then single out the positive aspects of it in regard to the individual doing it. Encouragement requires parents to go an extra mile because it forces them to be proactive. Here are some specific ways you can encourage your teen.

With Words

In healthy relationships, verbal affirmation is never redundant. Each of us enjoys receiving a pat on the back or hearing "well done" from someone we respect. We appreciate hearing how our actions pleased or helped another. Teens are no different. Like the rest of us, they are powerfully encouraged when justifiable praise comes their way.

If you are not verbalizing your encouragement, what message are you sending? Verbally encourage your teens in the little things and the big. It's easier to catch their big efforts, but many times it's the daily stuff that makes or breaks relationships. Sometimes a simple "thank you" can go a long way.

Another way to verbally encourage a child is to say, "I need your help," instead of "I want it," or just "Do this." Humbly asking for help elevates the person whose help is being sought.

If you are just getting started on the encouragement side of your relationship, be careful not to qualify your encouragement.

Don't say, "Thanks for doing the dishes tonight. Miracles never cease," or "You prepared a great meal; too bad it's burnt." Such qualified encouragement is not encouragement at all.

With Touch

The touch of a gentle hand, a tender hug, or a pat on the back can convey a message of encouragement. Physical encouragement communicates support, whether in victory or defeat. It fills in when words fail or aren't enough.

To hold and be held communicates vulnerability and a closeness that is reserved for trusting members of a family. Those with a struggling relationship with their teens may need to start slowly by simply placing a hand on a son's or daughter's shoulder and saying, "Great game," "Great job," or "Thank you." At other times, a high-five or a hug may be best. Whatever the case, don't underestimate the powerful influence of physical encouragement on your teenage son or daughter.

Anne Marie has always been great at combining words of encouragement and simple but meaningful expressions of physical touch. Sometimes she would just stop the kids, put her hands on their shoulders, and with great sincerity say, "I just want you to know how much I appreciate the way you...." Verbal affirmation combined with physical touch are an unbeatable combination.

There is a tendency to use the encouragement of touch only when we're happy. But believe me, if we'd had a bad day, our teens would notice when we put a gentle hand on their shoulders to say so. Consciously or unconsciously, they'd register the added emotional effort that the gesture cost.

Gift-Giving

Teens relish being appreciated. One way to show this is through gift-giving. Giving a gift in response to a child's act of loving service is a great way to remind the child that you have not forgotten what he or she did.

We have tried to practice spontaneous gift-giving in our home. There were occasions when my wife and I rushed out the door to a meeting, leaving the kitchen in disarray. Coming home to a spotless kitchen without having prompted the girls to clean up created in us a desire to express our appreciation with more than a simple "thank you." The next day Anne Marie would pick up a couple of thank you cards and write the girls a note of thanks on behalf of the two of us. Sometimes she would slip an inexpensive pair of earrings in with each card.

This cost very little time or money, yet it communicated our deep appreciation for our daughters' kindness and our desire to celebrate our love for them. It also added quality the next time we said, "Thank you."

Whether you are working on reclaiming a relationship with your teen or just working to improve it, consider saying "I appreciate you" with a simple gift. However, try to avoid some common pitfalls. Don't attach any strings or conditions to your gift. Don't do it just because the idea is in this book. Make it a genuine gift from your heart. Don't give with expectations. If you find yourself saying, "How could you do that after I gave you...?" realize you're giving with expectations. And don't use it as a defense during later conflicts.

With Service

Closely associated with gift-giving is saying thank you through acts of service. In the kitchen-cleaning incident, we could also have expressed our thanks by doing something for the kids that we knew they would appreciate—something over and above what we would normally do.

The teen years were hectic in our home, and there were times when the girls' rooms showed it. Although the girls often kept them neat, there were seasons of clutter. Sometimes during these busy times, Anne Marie would clean their rooms. She wanted to say, "I love and appreciate you" in a tangible way. That act of service communicated the value we placed on what our children were giving to our lives. We appreciated it, and they knew it.

Quality Time

A fifth way to show encouragement to our teens is by giving them our time. As parents, we all struggle to balance competing demands. Work quotas, family responsibilities, personal interests, friendships, ministry opportunities, personal interests—all these and more cry out for our attention.

Your teen is probably well aware of the battle you wage—after all, he or she lives with you. Better than anyone else, your family knows how little time you have to spare. With that in mind, what could be more encouraging than to show up to cheer at your child's drama production, band concert, or soccer game? Or you could take your teen to lunch one day to demonstrate your appreciation for a special act such as helping a younger brother with his homework, making peace with a friend, or fixing dinner the night mom was sick.

These are just some of the many ways we can encourage our kids. But don't let the suggestions we've outlined limit you. Remember, any action that you do as a parent that instills in your teen the courage to do right is encouragement.

Now, let's take a look at the role of correction in the moral training of our teens.

QUESTIONS FOR REVIEW

1. Look back on how you've disciplined your teen in the past week. Was it all corrective? Write down two times you could have used encouragement to discipline.

2. The literal meaning of the word encouragement is "to put courage in." Why do you think your son or daughter needs courage to live morally?

3. Describe one example of nonmoral behavior that you witnessed in your teen during the past week. Write an instance of moral behavior.

4. Which method of encouragement (words, touch, gifts, service, time) do you find easiest to use? Which method is the most difficult for you? What is one thing you can do this week to practice the most difficult method? the easiest?

5. Describe one way you can encourage each of your teenagers this week. Remember to make your encouragement individual and sincere.

CHAPTER THIRTEEN

Disciplining Your Teen

The frustration on their faces matched these parents' words: "How do we discipline our son? Everything we've tried doesn't work. We just don't know what to do anymore. He's too old to spank and too young to let go his own way."

We can't count how many times we've listened to parents struggling with disciplining their teenagers. Sometimes parents get the mistaken idea that if they figure out how to punish, that will "fix" every problem. As we go through this chapter, remember that correction is only one part of the moral-training (discipline) process. And that discipline is most effective in the context of a healthy parent-teen relationship. Don't expect correction to fix all teen problems, but view it as a God-given tool for maintaining our hearts.

GOVERNING PRINCIPLES

The reason we bring correction into the lives of our teens is basic. Correction helps teens learn. But in order for the correction to be tied to learning, we need to understand two important governing principles.

The first is this: The type of correction depends on the presence or absence of an evil motive. Parents should ask, "Was my teen's wrong action accidental or intentional? The answer to that question determines which type of correction is appropriate. This is the dividing line. Bad decisions and accidents bring natural consequences; intentional moral violations affecting other people require punishment. There is a difference between bringing consequences into the life of your teen and punishing your teen.

As parents, we need to understand punishment from a biblical perspective, not a societal one. Society punishes to get even and to exact revenge; God does not. He is not vindictive, nor does He seek to even the score. His purpose for punitive correction is precise. It is to bring about the "peaceable fruit of righteousness" (Hebrews 12:11).

In adulthood, we are not punished for our decisions; instead, we learn life's lessons by living with the correctness or incorrectness of our choices. So should it be with our teens. Because your teen is closer to adulthood than childhood, the need for punishment should sharply drop, while the use of natural and logical consequences becomes the more common method employed during correction.

The second rule of correction is this: *The punishment/consequences must fit the crime.* Punishment sets a value on behavior. That is why over-punishing or under-punishing is dangerous. Both send the wrong message.

When we as a society—or as parents—establish a punishment, we are making a value statement. We are determining the degree and seriousness of a wrongful act. Punishment places a value on the action. It is important to note that a child's sense of justice is established through punishment, not rewards. For example, if a child hits and bruises his sister with a plastic bat and then is punished by receiving five minutes in the timeout chair, the parent has just established in the mind of the child that hurting other people is not that serious an infraction.

Unjust punishments can go to the other extreme, too. When a parent says, "You left your light on after leaving your room. For that, you can't play your radio for a month," he is over-punishing his child. This fosters exasperation and more conflict.

Before an offense can be dealt with most effectively, the parent needs to ask two questions: "Was what my child did the result of an accident, or was it malicious? What punishment would fit the wrong and convey the right value message?"

TEENISHNESS OR FOOLISHNESS?

Discerning the intent or motive of your teen may seem like an impossible task. Parents may be asking, "How can I use the governing principle of motive, if I don't know what my teen's motive was?" Sometimes we cannot know, at least at first. But it helps to realize our sons' and daughters' wrong behavior will either be *foolish* or *teenish*.

From time to time we all act inappropriately. Sometimes we plan to do wrong, but there are times when we make honest mistakes, too. One wrong behavior is intentional; the other is not. The same is true of our young children and teens.

Willful defiance and open rebellion are what the Bible calls foolishness. Proverbs 22:15 tells us that "foolishness is bound up in the heart of a child." The word in this verse comes from the root word *folly,* which means deception, trickery, disobedience, lack of wisdom, or rebellion. The Bible says foolish acts are rebellious acts.

On the other hand, honest mistakes are just that: mistakes with no ill will attached. When our daughter accidentally tripped on the lamp cord, breaking the porcelain lamp, she didn't do it on purpose. There was no evil intent on her part, no associated disobedience, and no willful defiance. She accidentally tripped.

When young children make honest mistakes we label the

behavior *childishness*. When teens make honest mistakes we call it *teenishness*. Both childishness and teenishness refer to mistakes made in the absence of ill motives. Although there is no intent to do wrong, correction still needs to be applied. Our daughter had to face an admonishment or some consequences, even though she did not intentionally do wrong. The consequence, which we will discuss in a moment, was not given as a punishment, but to help her understand that personal responsibility is a prerequisite to freedom. Consequences for honest mistakes are not the same as consequences and punishment brought on as a result of open defiance.

Admonishment

Correcting teenish behavior begins with admonishment (Ephesians 6:4). The word *admonishment* means to put into one's mind or to warn. Admonishment, then, is to warn the teen that an action, or lack of action, is unwise and that it may bring calamity to the teen or others.

Ben is a conscientious teenager who usually takes his mountain bike into the house when he is finished riding it. But one day, in a rush to share some news with his mom, Ben dropped his bike in the front yard and ran into the house. He forgot about it. When his father came home, he found the bike in the front yard.

Was Ben wrong for leaving his bike on the front lawn? Yes. Was it done with the motive to disobey? No. It was a teenish act—maybe not smart, but certainly not evil. For that rare offense, his dad admonished him to be sure to put the bike in a safe place each time he finished riding. That warning served to encourage Ben to be responsible. If Ben's dad were to find the bicycle in the front yard the next day, he might apply certain consequences related to Ben's failure to be responsible even after a warning.

Related Consequences

Some mistakes bypass the warning stage and require immediate consequences. Those consequences need to be logical and related to the mistake. The purpose of consequences is to encourage good stewardship and to cause the teen to accept responsibility for nonrebellious yet unwise actions. When mistakes come, they are usually associated with property, privileges, and personal behavior. Immediate consequences eliminate future evil, according to Solomon (Ecclesiastes 8:11).

Teaching a teen how to be a good steward of his or her own possessions will help him or her to be responsible with others' property. Let's return to our story of Ben and his bike. A couple of days after the first incident, Ben left his bike near the front porch while he went into the house—just to retrieve his jacket, he thought. Once inside, he got caught in an unexpected phone conversation. Ben hadn't realized how easy it is to get sidetracked!

He didn't intend to ignore his father's counsel of two days earlier, but he took an unwise chance, believing he would be in the house for only a minute. When his dad arrived home and found the bike, he took it away for a couple of days; he had moved to the second level of correction by applying related consequences. That response helped Ben learn that with the privilege of riding a bicycle comes the responsibility of taking care of it.

Explanations should always accompany stewardship training. As your child grows, however, the explanations should get briefer. By the time Ben is fifteen years old, he more than likely already knows his bike could get stolen or rust in bad weather if left out. Dad doesn't need to go into these reasons in depth. All he needs to say is something such as "Ben, in your haste, you're forgetting that your bike could be taken or ruined if left outside. To help remind you, I'll hang on to it for two days."

Parents should hold teens personally responsible for their nonrebellious accidents that affect other people or others' property. Let's return to the example of our daughter and the lamp cord. Although she hadn't meant to break the lamp, it happened. We implemented related consequences to teach her to accept responsibility for her mistakes and to help her learn to make things right. Based on her age, we required her to do additional chores around the house to earn enough money to help pay for replacing the broken lamp.

Making restitution was part of the consequences. We required payment of her. We didn't do this because we needed the money; we did it because we wanted her to understand the concepts of labor, money, property value, and personal responsibility. We wanted her to see how they all fit together.

A parent can also structure related consequences to help a teen be responsible with a privilege. Heidi had an opportunity to earn some extra money. To do this, she was required to work three hours each day after school. Her parents consented with the stipulation that her grades must not suffer. When her next report card came out, her parents saw that their daughter's grades had slipped. As a result, Heidi had to give up the privilege of working after school until she brought her grades back up. Every error a child makes, intentional or not, can be seen as an opportunity to teach morally responsible behavior. But if the offense is intentional, it must be dealt with differently.

THE FOOL'S CHOICE

Proverbs 19:18 says, "Chasten your son while there is hope, and do not set your heart on his destruction." The destruction Solomon speaks of is the type that comes as the result of parental neglect or lack of training.

Parents who have teens in trouble are often discouraged to

the point of giving up. But this verse says, in essence, "Hang in there, parents; persevere for the sake of your child." There is still hope. But don't skip over Solomon's warning. If you fail to correct when correction is needed, you will be abandoning your child to his destruction. Those are strong words, and they are right words. Don't give up; keep pursuing. The relationship is too important to neglect. Continue striving to "stir up love and good works" in your child (Hebrews 10:24).

Living with the mistakes our kids make is much easier than living with the consequences of their rebellion. In the case of a mistake, you are dealing with an objective, measurable action. However, with rebellion you are facing something much more complex: your teen's subjective motivation. This is all the more reason to be clear about this aspect of correction.

When we talk about discipline, the real issue is leadership, not punishment. That's not to say we should abandon the type of consequence that puts a value on a misdeed, but that our focus should be on elevating good, not simply suppressing evil. It's not one or the other. It's both.

Foolish behavior needs correction, but parents shouldn't correct all foolishness in the same way or with the same strength of consequences. It's natural for all of us to react spontaneously to negative behavior, but we should suppress that natural tendency and carefully consider our reactions. What criteria should we consider when setting consequences? Where should we begin when our teens are in need of correction?

FOUR CONSIDERATIONS

Before determining the consequences of foolish or rebellious behavior, it is important to consider these four factors.

What punishment would fit the offense? When considering consequences, parents should remember that punishment that is too harsh exasperates the teen and that punishment that is too lenient fails to put a correct value on the offense.

How frequent is the offense? Since we know offenses range from infrequent, minor infractions to frequent episodes of open defiance, correction should reflect the frequency of the offense. A first-time episode should be handled differently from a third one.

What is the context of the moment? Context is not an excuse for rebellion, but it should be taken into consideration when determining consequences. Consider what incited the incident to determine context. In Chapter 11 we gave the example of a teen who was asked to turn off a video game right before it ended. It would be wrong for him to refuse, but the frustration that led to his poor behavior would be normal.

What is the overall behavior of the teen? Is foolishness rare, growing more frequent, or a regular pattern? This consideration is especially helpful if society's expectations about the teen years have made a parent fearful. A parent might then view a single rebellious act as a precursor of worse behavior and come down too hard.

THREE LEVELS

After you have identified foolish or rebellious behavior and have considered these four factors, you can then determine the appropriate level of consequence. When considering the consequence, it is important to remember that punishment that is too harsh exasperates the teen; punishment that is too lenient fails to put a correct value on the offense. In order to prevent over-punishment or under-punishment, you need to understand how to assess your teen's wrongful actions and determine into which level of correction they fall. Generally, teenage foolishness falls into one of three levels of correction.

Level One: Minor Infractions

The first level of offense calls for a *verbal warning* only. Most of the time, teens who most often require this level of correction would be classified, both within the family and by the public, as a "good kid." The fact that a teen receives only a warning for the infraction does not reduce the significance of the wrong action or the need for compliance, but you wouldn't punish a teen for a single infraction if he or she is normally characterized by compliance.

For example, let's say your teen disobeyed by staying out an hour past curfew without calling first. And let's say this was the first time in six months that it has happened. In this case, while the behavior may still be an infraction according to the letter of the law, it does not require the full weight of punishment. Instead, the fair weight of justice needs to be brought into perspective. You should consider a teen's actions at this first level in light of his or her normal overall behavior. Your son or daughter is simply not characterized by breaking curfew. Therefore, a simple verbal reminder or reprimand is sufficient.

Considering the circumstances and the teen's normal pattern of behavior, any applied consequence greater than a warning might prove devastating to a teen's motivation for achieving moral excellence. Teens become exasperated when parents pursue perfection and not excellence, especially since mom and dad themselves are not perfect parents.

Level Two: Infractions That Require Action

The next level of offenses call for *action with verbal correction*. These kinds of offenses include new behaviors that are becoming more common, old habits that are reemerging, or yesterday's warning that has not been heeded.

One action that parents with younger children and younger

teens can use is a "reflective timeout." Proverbs 22:3 states, "A prudent man foresees evil and hides himself, but the simple pass on and are punished." A reflective period forces a teen to stop what he or she is doing and think. The teen is instructed to sit, not as a punishment, but as a time to get control of thoughts and actions and to think about the course he or she is on before the behavior leads to harsher consequences.

A timeout is the last stop before crossing the bridge to trouble. The idea is to get the teen to ask, *Do I really want to go in that direction?* Whether it involves a new behavior or a reemerging old habit, you are calling attention to the behavior and letting the teen make the decision to do what is right. If he or she fails to respond properly, the behavior automatically becomes a level-three offense.

Level Three: Offenses That Require the Full Weight of the Law

The third level of offense refers to routine acts and attitudes of defiance that are both active and passive and to moral violations against others including siblings, peers, parents, and those in authority. This third level of offense involves different types of applied consequences which include natural and logical consequences, loss of privileges, and restitution. Spanking or use of the rod as the Bible speaks of it, is neither appropriate nor an effective method of correction during the teen years. We would not recommend it.

CONSEQUENCES

Rebellious and defiant acts sometimes produce their own pain as a natural outcome. Do you remember our story about Ben and his bike? Let's suppose the bike was stolen. The natural consequence of Ben's disobedience to his father's instruction is the loss of a valuable bicycle. To replace his bike, he would have to find a job, which might require that he give up ballgames and other fun on weekends. The price Ben would pay for his disobedience would be high indeed!

There are two things we want to accomplish with correction. First, we want to help our teens take ownership of their decisions, and second, we want to help them learn how to make wise decisions. That, of course, comes with moral maturity. The most effective way to bring attention to poor decisions is to allow teens to live with the consequences of their choices.

Another form of correction is the use of logical consequences. The consequence a parent employs should be logically associated with the offense if no natural consequence serves the corrective purpose.

Suppose a thirteen-year-old ignores his parents' instruction to go directly home after school. Instead, he visits with a friend, forgetting that his parents were planning to take him out to buy new baseball spikes after school. The parents have only a forty-five-minute block of time in which to make the purchase; after that, they are committed elsewhere.

What is the logical consequence of this boy's disobedience: take away his computer game, make him go without supper, or assign him extra chores around the house? No. None of those consequences is logically associated with the boy's foolishness. Not getting to go pick up the baseball spikes he wants is the logical consequence of his wrong actions.

Consequential Training Has Limits

A father once remarked, "If I didn't keep constant pressure on my kid, he would never do his homework. No homework, no good grades; no good grades, no college; no college, no future. If I let him live with the consequences of his own choices, then he will ruin his life."

This is both a logical and legitimate concern. Because some consequences for bad decisions made as a teenager are so devastating now and in the future, we cannot simply let the law of consequences direct our teenagers. While we believe teens should live with the consequences of their own decisions, we do not believe they should make all the decisions. Parents need to be proactively working with their teens to make the right decisions rather than waiting to find the right consequences that will help them in the future. One consequence of a bad decision may be that your teenager has no future.

Loss of Privilege

The loss of a privilege is another option to draw your teen's attention to a foolish action. Suppose your fourteen-year-old spends his afternoons at a friend's house next door. He knows dinner is at six o'clock but shows up ten minutes late every night. Losing the privilege of going to his friend's house is both logical and necessary. With privilege comes responsibility. Being responsible with one's time is a form of responsibility.

When employing this consequence, don't focus only on your child's loss of a privilege; focus also on the importance of being responsible with privileges. Remember, you are attempting to reach your child's heart, not simply punish bad behavior.

Restitution

Restitution is a biblical concept defined as repayment for lost, damaged, or stolen property. The principle of restitution was very much a part of American Judeo-Christian ethics thirty years ago. If you broke a friend's cookie jar, you bought a new one. If your child broke a neighbor's window, you replaced it.

Whenever financial liability occurs as a result of mistakes or intentional wrongdoing, restitution should be part of the restoration process. Old Testament law required restitution when intentional or unintentional acts caused property damage or loss. In Exodus 22, Moses delineates how and why this method worked (see verses 1, 3, 5, 6, and 12). The practice of providing restitution was documented in the New Testament, too. When speaking with Jesus, Zacchaeus said, "If I have taken anything from anyone by false accusation, I restore fourfold" (Luke 19:8).

Saying "I'm sorry" and asking for forgiveness are not enough when our teens' actions create a financial liability. Their age and full understanding of the value of a dollar make restitution a great teacher of what it is to be a responsible human being.

ONE WARNING

We know that consistent rules that are fairly administered make submitting to parental leadership attractive—even to a teenager. We also know the health of the parent-teen relationship determines whether the teen accepts the parents' right to lead, encourage, and correct.

Discipline during the teen years is a function of parental relationship, not parental power. Keep working on that relationship. Success is not measured by getting your teen to mind you as much as getting your teen to follow you.

QUESTIONS FOR REVIEW

1. Name a teenish act your son or daughter did recently. Name a foolish act.

2. Describe a situation in which your teen might benefit from a "reflective timeout."

3. It is difficult not to react spontaneously to foolish or rebellious actions. Make an acrostic or some other clue to help you remember the four things you need to consider before responding to foolishness.

4. Review the types of consequences. Which is the hardest for you to employ? Why?

5. Take a moment to think about our final warning. Write down one thing you can do tomorrow to let your teenager know that you love him or her.

CHAPTER FOURTEEN

The Discovery Continues

Betty Brooks and Tommy Snooks were leaving church one Sunday. Said Betty Brooks to Tommy Snooks, "Well, tomorrow will be Monday." Betty Brooks knew what we as parents must understand: At some point theory must express itself in practice. Good ideas if they are not fleshed out into everyday, rubber-meets-the-road stuff are just that—good ideas and nothing more. Even Betty Brooks understood that.

We are not attempting to merely fill your head and your teen's head with new ideas and clever-sounding theories. It is our hope that our teaching will lead to changed lives, parents and teens who will lift high the glory of God. God will be glorified when His creation proceeds along that course which leads back to His original design. Christ came to reveal, redeem, and restore. In effect, whether or not Monday morning is different in your home is the true test of success.

If there is one word that can sum up a final charge to our readers, it is the word *discovery*. By discovery, we mean the restoration of God's creation, the family, and more specifically, parents and teens, to the intended beauty of His original design. In other words, parenting teenagers isn't just something that life throws our way; therefore, we must simply learn to deal with it in the best way possible. The guiding principle of parenting, contrary to popular belief, is not pragmatic. Rather, we believe the Bible teaches that all life, including parent-teen relationships, must be viewed from a heavenly perspective. Nothing, including this relationship, stands outside the call of God upon His creation to give Him glory (1 Corinthians 10:31).

Certainly, some people in our day use the term *discovery* to refer to the need to awaken the sleeping giant of human potential which supposedly, as the humanistic line of thinking goes, resides in all of us. But godliness is not a matter of dogged human endeavor. It is not achievable by skipping over the centrality of Christ. Right behavior is a consequence of a right relationship with God. Thus, to us, the term *discovery* means living a life of complete devotion to and dependence upon God. It means to know God, to love Him with all your heart, mind, and soul.

The dynamic of family discovery assumes three very important truths. First, it assumes the supremacy of God's grace. At the core of Christianity is an understanding that life is not first a matter of us doing something for God but rather God doing something in us. The former slave trader turned preacher, John Newton, wrote a hymn in 1779 which has become a Christian classic. Churchgoers and unbelievers alike know and sing the song. In fact, it is one of the most familiar and most recorded songs in history. Of course, we are speaking of "Amazing Grace," which opens with these words:

> Amazing grace! How sweet the sound
> That saved a wretch like me!
> I once was lost but now am found,
> Was blind, but now I see.

Above and beyond all else, parents and teens need the grace of God. Ultimately, everything comes back to trusting in God's grace for regeneration and sanctification. Keep grace at the center of your family. Without it, nothing else matters. Grace truly is amazing.

Second, discovery assumes the need to be renewed in our thinking. Remember the apostle Paul's familiar words in Romans 12:2: "Do not be conformed to this world, but be transformed by the renewing of your mind." Parents and teens alike enter the kingdom of God with a mind that needs transforming. Natural parenting—doing what feels right—leads to disaster. Because of sin, what feels right to the mind when it is not under the control of the Holy Spirit and not under the authority of the Word of God is wickedness. The mind needs renewal. In Ephesians 4:17–24 as well as in many other places in the Bible, we learn that there is an inexorable connection between right thinking and right behaving. If Christ is to be seen in the way we live, He must be at the center of the way we think. Discovery means learning something new. It means allowing God to align our thinking with the character of Christ. The minds of parents and the minds of teens must be aimed in the direction of God.

Third, discovery assumes that growth is a process. Keep in mind that process is God's idea. Because it is God's idea, we have the assurance that He is glorified in process though the process will at times include discouragement and defeat. God is glorified in our weakness. We may not understand it, but God is glorified more through gradual growth, which will by definition include ups and downs, than He would be in instant and complete growth. God could make us like Christ the instant He saves us, but He chooses not to do so. We think it is because God is most glorified in us when we are most dependent upon Him. You will not experience instant success in your parent-teen relationship no matter how faithful you are to the task. You will not be exempt from heartache and pain. But rather than discouraging you, that ought to fill your soul to the brim with hope. The God we love and serve is bigger than our problems. He is so great that He can take the ugliest situation and turn it to our good (Romans 8:28).

To any teenager reading these words, we say: What an opportunity you have to help God change your parents! Your parents are not yours by some consequence of blind chance. God gave your parents to you. What is more, He gave you to your parents. You have each other so that God's grace and love will be made large through your relationship. You cannot be all that God wills for you to be without your parents. That is not a new thought to you, we know. But maybe this is new: Do you realize that your parents cannot be what God wills them to be without you? God is using you to shape your parents into the people He wants them to be—not just better parents but better human beings.

Our sovereign and loving Lord graciously gave you to your parents and your parents to you for the furtherance of His will and glory. Wow! Our God is truly a great God. Can you do anything less than completely entrust your life and situation to a loving Father whose power and compassion are without measure? We think not! Remember, the apostle Paul was knocked down but not knocked out; he was pressed but not pinned. Our God is a God of grace, of hope, of renewal. No matter how dark your darkness is, God is able to do abundantly, exceedingly above all we ask or think. God is in the healing and restoring business.

To parents we say: Do problems with your teenager seem hopeless? Is your situation so complex that you don't know where to start rebuilding? Is your sense of injury so deep that reconciliation seems impossible? Is your child so wayward that you fear permanent separation? If so, we humbly suggest that your God may be too small. After the apostle Paul speaks of our emancipation from the bondage of sin in Romans 6 and our freedom from the Law in chapter 7, he speaks of our freedom from fear in chapter 8. Because of God's great mercy which He bestows upon us through Christ, we need not fear condemnation (8:1). We need not fear separation from the love of God (8:31–39). Sandwiched between those two precious promises and comprising the rest of the chapter is the truth that we need not fear our weaknesses (8:2–30). God has made the provisions necessary to keep us walking in step with the Spirit. Don't allow the world, your flesh, and the devil to discourage you because of your failures. Remember, God's grace shines brightest in the darkest hour. Don't allow your fears to hinder the discovery process which God wills for you. Keep on growing in your knowledge of what God intends parenting to be. Allow the tension between what you know ought to be and what you know is in reality to cause you to turn to God. Cling as though your life depends upon it (and it does) to the promise that God will continue His work of grace in you. Men fail. God never fails.

While you may not necessarily understand all that God does, you must love and trust Him. He is worthy of your trust because He is in complete control of all things (1 Chronicles 29:11–12; Psalm 24:1; 115:3; 135:6). The sovereignty of God should solicit praise and submission from your heart. The God who works His will through earthquakes (Job 9:6), famine (Amos 4:6), and other calamities (Exodus 9:1–4) is able to work His will through your situation. Work in cooperation with God, not in opposition. Do not pray, "Lord, make my child a better person," but rather, "Lord, make me a better person." Every step of humility before our God and our children serves as a powerful, spiritual, magnetic force drawing our children closer to us. Family renewal starts in our hearts. "Search me, O God, and know my heart" (Psalm 139:23).

The discovery of the beauty of God's creation lies before you.

204 REACHING THE HEART OF YOUR TEEN

As you proceed along this path, keep in mind that God is on your side. He loves you. His grace is sufficient for you. His Word is a light and a path to guide you. His strength is greater than your weakness. His glory is all that matters. What wonder and joy are ours when we walk with God!

The Bible tells us in Judges 13 that the wife of Manoah "was barren and had no children" (verse 2). God graciously gave Manoah's wife a vision of the preincarnate Christ to tell her the thrilling news that she would have a son (verse 3). After the "angel of the Lord" left, she told her husband of the message the angel had given her. Then in verse 8 we read, "Manoah prayed to the LORD, and said, 'O my Lord, please let the Man of God whom You sent come to us again and teach us what we shall do for the child who will be born.'" What a precious prayer! We hope that is your prayer. It is our prayer for you.

NOTES

1. Art Levin, "The Second Time Around Realities of Remarriage," *U.S. News and World Report* (29 January 1990), 50.

2. G. Stanley Hall, *Adolescence* (New York: Appleton, 1904).

3. James S. Coleman, *The Adolescent Society* (New York: Free Press, 1961).

4. Erick Erikson, *Identity: Youth in Crisis* (New York: Norton, 1968).

5. Anna Freud, "Adolescence," *The Psychoanalytic Study of the Child* 13 (1958), 255–78.

6. S. Safari and M. Stern, *The Jewish People in the First Century* (Philadelphia: Fortress Press, 1987), 772–73.

7. Judith Swihart, *How to Say "I Love You"* (Downer's Grove, Ill.: Intervarsity Press, 1972), presents the core concepts that are found in Chapter 8. We also offer many thanks to Dr. Gary Chapman for his additional insights and practical applications. We highly recommend his book, *The Five Love Languages* (Chicago: Northfield Press, 1992), for a more complete discussion of this topic.

SUBJECT INDEX